1 and 2 Thessalonians
Discipleship Lessons

and Bible Study Commentary for Personal Devotional Use, Small Groups or Sunday School Classes, and Sermon Preparation for Pastors and Teachers

JesusWalk® Bible Study Series

by Dr. Ralph F. Wilson
Director, Joyful Heart Renewal Ministries

Additional books, and reprint licenses are available at:
www.jesuswalk.com/books/thessalonians.htm

Free Participant Guide handout sheets are available at:
www.jesuswalk.com/thessalonians/thessalonians-lesson-handouts.pdf

JesusWalk® Publications
Loomis, California

Paperback
ISBN-13: 978-0-9847340-7-8
ISBN-10: 0984734074

Library of Congress Control Number: 2012923802
Library of Congress subject headings:
        Bible. – N.T. – Thessalonians – Commentaries.
Suggested Classifications
        Library of Congress: BS2725.53
        Dewey Decimal System: 227.81

Published by JesusWalk® Publications, P.O. Box 565, Loomis, CA 95650-0565, USA.

JesusWalk is a registered trademark and Joyful Heart is a trademark of Joyful Heart Renewal Ministries.

130102

Preface

The church at Thessalonica in Macedonia is a newly planted congregation, located in the capital of the province. It is under fierce attack. Opposing Jewish leaders have caused a riot and driven the church-planting team out of town. To keep the peace, secular leaders have exacted a promise that the Apostle Paul won't return. But amazingly, against all odds, the new congregation begins to grow and attract converts from the pagan population of the city. What's more, it becomes a model congregation for the fledging Christian movement in the Mediterranean region.

1 and 2 Thessalonians, written about 50 AD – the earliest documents in the New Testament – reveal Paul's heart and passion as he seeks to guide this congregation towards health and balance.

In 1 and 2 Thessalonians we'll examine:

- God's grace in selecting his children,
- The heart and character of a disciple-maker,
- Christ's coming, the rapture, and the Antichrist,
- How to deal with overly-dependent members,
- A high view of sexual purity, and
- Keys to a healthy Christian congregation.

This study covers the two letters in nine lessons. Each lesson contains 4 or 5 discussion questions to help you or a group come to grips with the letters' teachings and the implications of these for your life.

My prayer is that you grow stronger as disciples as a result of this intensive study of 1 and 2 Thessalonians.

Dr. Ralph F. Wilson
January 1, 2013
Loomis, California

P.S. If you have purchased a book version, would you please be so kind as to write a two or three sentence review on the Amazon.com site? I would *really* appreciate it!

Table of Contents

References and Abbreviations

BDAG — Walter Bauer and Frederick William Danker, *A Greek-English Lexicon of the New Testament and Other Early Christian Literature*, (Third Edition; based on previous English editions by W.F. Arndt, F.W. Gingrich, and F.W. Danker; University of Chicago Press, 1957, 1979, 2000)

Bruce — F.F. Bruce, *1 & 2 Thessalonians* (Word Biblical Commentary 45; Word, 1982)

DPL — Gerald F. Hawthorne, Ralph P. Martin, and Daniel G. Reid (editors), *Dictionary of Paul and His Letters* (InterVarsity Press, 1993)

ISBE — Geoffrey W. Bromiley (general editor), *The International Standard Bible Encyclopedia* (Eerdmans, 1979-1988; fully revised from the 1915 edition)

KJV — King James Version (Authorized Version, 1611)

Kreeft and Tacelli, *Handbook* — Peter Kreeft and Ronald K. Tacelli, *Handbook of Christian Apologetics* (InterVarsity Press, 1994)

Liddell-Scott — Henry George Liddell. Robert Scott, *A Greek-English Lexicon* (revised and augmented throughout by Sir Henry Stuart Jones with the assistance of Roderick McKenzie; Oxford, Clarendon Press, 1940, Perseus Project online edition)

Metzger — Bruce M. Metzger, *A Textual Commentary on the Greek New Testament* (United Bible Societies, 1971)

Morris — Leon Morris, *The Epistles of Paul to the Thessalonians* (Tyndale New Testament Commentary, 1956)

NASB   New American Standard Bible (The Lockman Foundation, 1960-1988)

NIV   New International Version (International Bible Society, 1973, 1978)

NJB   New Jerusalem Bible (Darton, Longman & Todd Ltd, 1985)

NRSV   New Revised Standard Version (Division of Christian Education of the National Council of Churches of Christ, USA, 1989)

Robertson   Archibald Thomas Robertson, *Word Pictures in the New Testament* (Sunday School Board of the Southern Baptist Convention, 1932, 1960)

Stott   John Stott, *The Gospel and the End of Time: The Message of 1 and 2 Thessalonians* (InterVarsity Press, 1991)

TDNT   Gerhard Kittel and Gerhard Friedrich (editors), Geoffrey W. Bromiley (translator and editor), *Theological Dictionary of the New Testament* (Eerdmans, 1964-1976; translated from *Theologisches Wörterbuch zum Neuen Testament*, ten volume edition)

Wanamaker   Charles A. Wanamaker, *Commentary on 1 and 2 Thessalonians* (New International Greek Testament Commentary; Eerdmans/Paternoster, 1990)

Reprint Guidelines

Copying the Handouts. In some cases, small groups or Sunday school classes would like to use these notes to study this material. That's great. An appendix provides copies of handouts designed for classes and small groups. There is no charge whatsoever to print out as many copies of the handouts as you need for participants.

Free Participant Guide handout sheets are available at:

www.jesuswalk.com/thessalonians/thessalonians-lesson-handouts.pdf

All charts and notes are copyrighted and must bear the line:

"Copyright © 2013, Ralph F. Wilson. All rights reserved. Reprinted by permission."

You may not resell these notes to other groups or individuals outside your congregation. You may, however, charge people in your group enough to cover your copying costs.

Copying the book (or the majority of it) in your congregation or group, you are requested to purchase a reprint license for each book. A Reprint License, $2.50 for each copy is available for purchase at

www.jesuswalk.com/books/thessalonians.htm

Or you may send a check to:

Dr. Ralph F. Wilson
JesusWalk Publications
PO Box 565
Loomis, CA 95650, USA

The Scripture says,

"The laborer is worthy of his hire" (Luke 10:7) and "Anyone who receives instruction in the word must share all good things with his instructor." (Galatians 6:6)

However, if you are from a third world country or an area where it is difficult to transmit money, please make a small contribution instead to help the poor in your community.

Introduction to 1 and 2 Thessalonians

When Paul and his mission band came to Thessalonica about 49 AD, it was one of the most important provincial capitals in the Roman Empire.

City of Thessalonica

The city of Thessalonica was founded about 315 BC – on or near the ancient town of Therma – by Cassander, a general under Alexander the Great, and later, king of Macedonia. The city was named for Cassander's wife, Alexander's half-sister Thessalonica, daughter of Philip II of Macedon. The city was located at the head of the Termaic Gulf, the best natural harbor on the Aegean Sea.

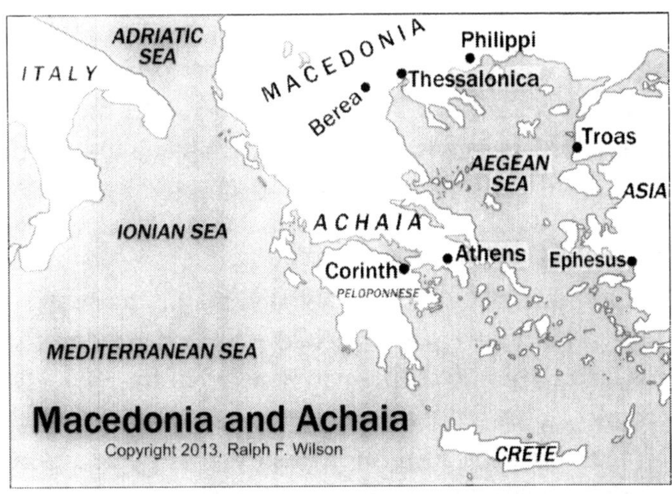

In 146 BC, Thessalonica became capital of the Roman province of Macedonia. In order to administer and protect its far-flung empire, Rome built a network of military highways. Thessalonica was on the Via Egnatia or Egnatian Way, completed in 146 BC, which connected Asia Minor with the Adriatic Sea (and Rome). It reached the Aegean Sea at Thessalonica. Like other major Roman roads, it was about 19.6 feet wide, and paved with large polygonal stone slabs or covered with a hard layer of sand.

Thessalonica became a free city in 42 BC and was the most important and largest city in Macedonia well into the third or fourth century AD. Today it is known as Salonika, the second largest city of modern Greece and an important seaport.

Founding of the Church in Thessalonica

We'll consider the founding of the church in Thessalonica in greater detail in Lesson 1, but here are the basics. According to Acts 17:1-10, Paul, Silas, and Timothy arrive at Thessalonica after leaving Philippi. Paul preaches at the Jewish synagogue in Thessalonica for several weeks, but as opposition develops, he leaves the synagogue to develop a congregation composed primarily of Gentiles. Jewish leaders succeed in stirring up a mob demanding that Paul and Silas be expelled from the city. In order to keep peace, city leaders extract promises and bonds from Jason, a prominent member of the new church, that Paul and Silas will not return. The apostles are secreted away that night under cover of darkness.

Date and Place of Origin

Paul goes first to Athens, then to Corinth, where he enjoys a successful 18-month ministry. During this time, Timothy visits Thessalonica and reports back to Paul good news about the church – as well as its problems. 1 Thessalonians was probably written from Corinth in the later part of 50 AD,[1] and 2 Thessalonians a few months later. 1 Thessalonians is written shortly after receiving a report from Timothy after a recent visit. 2 Thessalonians may have been prompted by a letter from the church.

Historical Situation and Purpose

Paul learns from Timothy several things that are reflected in his first letter. Opponents – both Jewish and secular – have degraded Paul's reputation. Part of 1 Thessalonians is to remind the Thessalonians what his character was when he was with them. He is rebuilding his reputation.

The church is suffering considerable persecution, but is increasing in love and good works. Unlike other Pauline churches, their chief problems don't seem to stem from external opponents corrupting their theology (though there may have been outside influence concerning their confusion about the Antichrist and Christ's coming). Paul brings strong correction to the loose sexual morals and over-dependency that is found among some members.

Paul's purpose in these letters is to encourage the new church through persecution, assure them of his character and love for them, and provide some correction in areas where they need it.

While some scholars believe that 2 Thessalonians was the first of the two letters written, there just isn't enough evidence to come to any firm conclusion. I accept the traditional order of the letters' writing.

---

[1] Bruce, *1&2 Thessalonians*, p. xxxv.

Authorship

Since earliest times, both 1 and 2 Thessalonians have been accepted as valid works of Paul, along with his associates Silas and Timothy. Some modern scholars have disputed Paul's authorship of 2 Thessalonians because of the degree of repetition and overlap, and a supposed difference in eschatology between the two letters. But neither argument seems to carry much weight. These letters are the authentic writings of Paul.

Silas and Timothy are named as co-authors in both letters, but the writing is probably Paul's. You probably know a lot about Paul, but here's some background on Silas and Timothy, two essential members of Paul's apostolic team.

Silas or Silvanus

We first see Silvanus or Silas (probably a contraction of Silvanus) as one of the "leading men among the brothers" in Jerusalem (Acts 15:22). He is selected to carry a letter from the Jerusalem Council to the Gentile churches. The letter conveys the amazing revelation that the Gentiles need not become Jews to be true Christians. They are only required to observe certain dietary customs to avoid offending their Jewish Christian brothers and sisters – and to avoid sexual immorality, which was rampant among non-Jews.

Later, Paul selects Silas to accompany him on his Second Missionary Journey, after Paul and Barnabas part company (Acts 15:36-41). Silas travels with Paul through Syria and the provinces of Cilicia, Galatia, and Asia. They are successful in the Macedonian city of Philippi but meet stiff opposition. Paul and Silas were stripped, flogged, and thrown in jail. But the Scripture records:

> "About midnight Paul and Silas were praying and singing hymns to God, and the other prisoners were listening to them." (Acts 16:25)

They are freed by an earthquake. The next city they come to was Thessalonica – and the rest is history. Silas is also mentioned as Paul's co-worker in Berea (Acts 17:14) and in Corinth (2 Corinthians 1:19). Robert C. Campbell observes,

> "Silas's ability to continue working in Berea after Paul was compelled to leave may indicate that he was less controversial than Paul."[2]

Probably it is this same Silas who serves as an amanuensis or secretary for the early church's other premier apostle, Simon Peter (1 Peter 5:12). Beyond that we know nothing about Silas.

---

[2] Robert C. Campbell, "Silas," ISBE 4:509.

Timothy

Timothy (whose name means "honoring God" or "venerating God") was born to a mixed marriage of a Jewish mother and a Greek, unbelieving father. His family lived in the city of Lystra.

On Paul's First Missionary Journey to this Lystra, Timothy, his mother Eunice, and his maternal grandmother Lois become believers (Acts 14:8-20; 2 Timothy 1:5). When Paul visits Lystra on his Second Missionary Journey (Acts 16:1-5), he recognizes the spiritual growth that has taken place in this young man in the intervening years.

Paul sees in Timothy the makings of an associate who can help him in his missionary endeavors. It may sound strange to us, but one of the qualifications Timothy had to meet in order to work with Paul was to be circumcised. Since Timothy was Jewish on his mother's side, he could hardly work with Paul in the synagogues of the Mediterranean as an uncircumcised Jew (Acts 16:3).

Timothy is probably commissioned by Paul and the elders in his home church of Lystra. There is a word of prophecy over him, the laying on of hands, and the impartation of a spiritual gift (1 Timothy 1:18; 4:14; 2 Timothy 1:6), perhaps that of evangelist (2 Timothy 4:5).

And so the partnership begins. Timothy travels with Paul's party as an assistant, apprentice, and protégé—and he gradually proves himself to be a trusted minister in his own right.

He travels with Paul and Silas to Philippi (Acts 16:12) and Berea (Acts 17:14), and joins Paul at Athens. Then he is sent to encourage the church in Thessalonica (1 Thessalonians 3:2) and later is with Paul and Silas in Corinth (1 Thessalonians 1:1; 2 Thessalonians 1:1).

On Paul's Third Missionary Journey, Timothy plays an important role, too. He is sent ahead to Philippi (Acts 19:22), then travels to meet Paul (1 Corinthians 16:10), is with Paul in Corinth (Romans 16:21), and travels with him to Philippi (Acts 20:3-6) before Paul returns to Jerusalem and imprisonment.

When Paul is sent in chains to Rome for trial, Timothy is there with him (Philippians 1:1; 2:19; Colossians 1:1; Philemon 1). He is a great comfort. Paul writes during this time:

> "I have no one else like him, who takes a genuine interest in your welfare. For everyone looks out for his own interests, not those of Jesus Christ. But you know that Timothy has proved himself, because as a son with his father he has served with me in the work of the gospel." (Philippians 2:20-22)

Later, Timothy spends some time in prison himself (Hebrews 13:23). After that his history gets fuzzy. Church tradition records that he serves as Bishop of Ephesus until 97 AD, when he is beaten to death and stoned by pagans at the age of about 80.[3]

[3] Eusebius, *Church History* III, 4, 6; *Apostolic Constitutions* VII, 46; and Nicephorus, *Church History*, III, 11.

1. The Secret of Bountiful Believers (1 Thessalonians 1:1-10)

The best place to begin our study of the Thessalonian epistles is to examine the historical context, the founding of the congregation probably only a year or so before these letters were written.

Paul's Second Missionary Journey

On his Second Missionary Journey, Paul had travelled through Asia Minor. Paul wasn't a "solo missionary," rather he operated with a small team – in this case it consisted of Paul, Silas, and Timothy.[4]

At Troas, Paul has a vision of a Man of Macedonia asking him to come and help them. He takes it as God's call, travelling to Macedonia and later to Greece (Achaia).

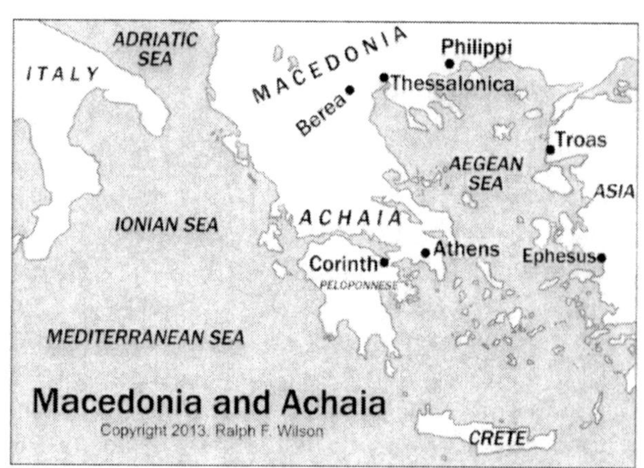

In Philippi he begins a church, but Paul and Silas end up being beaten and thrown in jail. They are released by means of an earthquake, convert their jailer and his family, but are still asked to leave by the city officials in the morning.

Founding the Church in Thessalonica (Acts 17:1-10)

Undeterred, Paul and his band continue south to Thessalonica.

"[1] When they had passed through[5] Amphipolis and Apollonia, they came to Thessalonica, where there was a Jewish synagogue. [2] As his custom[6] was, Paul went into the syna-

---

[4] Luke (who uses "we" to describe events) was clearly with the team in Philippi. But in Thessalonica, we're not sure.

[5] *Diodeuō*, "go, travel through" (BDAG 250, 1), "It means literally to make one's way (*hodos*) through (*dia*). They took the Egnatian Way..." (Robertson, *Word Pictures*).

gogue, and on three Sabbath days he reasoned with[7] them from the Scriptures, [3] explaining[8] and proving[9] that the Christ had to suffer and rise from the dead. 'This Jesus I am proclaiming to you is the Christ,' he said. [4] Some of the Jews were persuaded and joined Paul and Silas, as did a large number of God-fearing Greeks and not a few prominent women." (Acts 17:1-4)

"God-fearing Greeks" (NIV), or "devout Greeks" (NRSV, KJV) are non-Jews who were attracted to the synagogue because of the high morality expounded by Judaism. They are not full proselytes, however, since they typically stopped short of circumcision. To lose a "large number" of this group would have had a strong impact on the synagogue – and its finances.

Some of the converts are women of high rank, wives of city officials. However, most of the converts seem to have been Gentiles from the working class, and many of these are saved not from the synagogue, but directly from paganism (1:9). The Jews in Thessalonica are upset that Paul is attracting such a large following and seek to stop him.

"[5] But the Jews were jealous; so they rounded up some bad characters from the marketplace,[10] formed a mob[11] and started a riot[12] in the city. They rushed[13] to Jason's house in search of Paul and Silas in order to bring them out to the crowd. [6] But when they did not

---

[6] "Custom" (NIV, NRSV), "manner" is the verbal adjective *eithōs*, "to maintain a custom or tradition, be accustomed" (BDAG 295).

[7] "Reasoned with" (NIV, KJV), "argued with" is *dialegomai*, "'to engage in speech interchange, converse, discuss, argue,' especially of instructional discourse that frequently includes exchange of opinions" (BDAG 232, 1).

[8] "Explaining" (NIV, NRSV), "opening" (KJV) is *dianoigō*, "explain, interpret" the Scriptures (BDAG 234, 2). This is the same word used when Jesus explained the Scriptures to the men on the road to Emmaus after his resurrection (Luke 24:32, 45).

[9] "Proving" (NIV, NRSV), "alleging" (KJV) is *paratithēmi*, "to place something before someone, set before," here, to "set forth in teaching," middle voice, "demonstrate, point out" (BDAG 772, 2b). Here, the KJV "alleging" doesn't mean asserting without proof. Rather, allege is used in the archaic sense of "to adduce or bring forward as a source or authority" (Robertson, *Word Pictures*; *Merriam Webster Collegiate Dictionary*, 11th edition).

[10] "Bad characters" (NIV), "ruffians" (NRSV), "lewd fellows" (KJV) is two words: the plural of *anēr*, "man, male" and *ponēros*, "pertaining to being morally or socially worthless, wicked, evil, bad, base, worthless, vicious, degenerate," here "rowdies, ruffians" (BDAG 853, 1aα). The are described as *agoraios*, "market people," specifically, "the crowd in the market place," and so "rabble" (BDAG 14, 1).

[11] "Formed a mob" (NIV, NRSV), "gathered a company" (KJV) is *ochlopoieō*, "form a mob," not found elsewhere (BDAG 745), a compound verb from *ochlos*, "crowd, horde" + "*poieō*, "do, make."

[12] "Started a riot" (NIV), "set the city in an uproar" (NRSV, KJV) is *thorybeō*, "throw into disorder" (BDAG 458, 1).

[13] "Rushed to" (NIV), "attacked" (NRSV), "assaulted" (KJV) is *ephistēmi*, "stand at or near," here, with the specific sense of "to come near with intention of harming, attack" (BDAG 418, 3).

find them, they dragged[14] Jason and some other brothers before the city officials, shouting: 'These men who have caused trouble[15] all over the world have now come here, [7] and Jason has welcomed them into his house. They are all defying Caesar's decrees, saying that there is another king, one called Jesus.'" (Acts 17:5-7)

Notice that the Jews don't attack Paul directly. They find "some bad characters from the marketplace" to do their dirty work for them. An historical note helps us understand the charge made before the city officials. In this period, a militant messianic movement (different from Christianity) was spreading among Jewish communities. To stop the violence, in 49 AD Emperor Claudius expelled the Jews from Rome – which is why Aquila and Priscilla had recently moved from Rome to Corinth (Acts 18:2).

So when the mob accuses Paul and Silas of having "caused trouble all over the world" and "defying Caesar's decrees" with regard to a messiah figure, they are connecting Paul and Silas to the recent civil unrest among the Jews in Rome. That's why the Jews couldn't bring these charges themselves.[16]

> "[8] When they heard this, the crowd and the city officials were thrown into turmoil.[17]
> [9] Then they made Jason and the others post bond and let them go. [10] As soon as it was night, the brothers sent Paul and Silas away to Berea." (Acts 17:8-10a)

Jason is a prominent Jew who has converted to Christ, since elsewhere Paul seems to refer to him as a kinsman (Romans 16:21). The Greek name "Jason" was common among the Hellenistic Jews, who used it for "Jesus" or "Joshua."[18] Jason is apparently forced to put up money and pledge to the city officials that Paul and his band would leave the city and not cause further problems.

But the Thessalonian Jews don't stop there. They disrupt Paul's ministry in the next city, too.

> "When the Jews in Thessalonica learned that Paul was preaching the word of God at Berea, they went there too, agitating[19] the crowds and stirring them up. The brothers

---

[14] "Dragged" (NIV, NRSV), "drew" (KJV) is *syrō*, "drag, pull, draw, drag away" (BDAG 977).

[15] "Caused trouble" (NIV), "turn the world upside down" (NRSV, KJV) is *anastatoō*, "to upset the stability of a pers. or group, disturb, trouble, upset" (BDAG 72).

[16] See Bruce, *1&2 Thessalonians*, xxiii-xxiv.

[17] "Were thrown into turmoil" (NIV), "were disturbed" (NRSV), "troubled" (KJV) is *tarassō*, "shake together, stir up," here figurative, "to cause inward turmoil, stir up, disturb, unsettle, throw into confusion" (BDAG 990, 2).

[18] John Hutchison and S.F. Hunter, "Jason," ISBE 2:970.

[19] "Agitating" (NIV), "stir up" (NRSV, KJV) is *saleuō*, "shake," here, figuratively, "to disturb inwardly, disturb, shake" (BDAG 912, 2).

immediately sent Paul to the coast, but Silas and Timothy stayed at Berea." (Acts 17:13-14)

Paul travels to Athens and stays there for a time. Later he goes to the Greek city of Corinth, where he apparently writes the Thessalonian letters.

What follows is the first discussion question of this lesson series. Think deeply about the questions. If you go to the trouble of writing down your answers, it will help you form your answer carefully and thoughtfully. Then click on the web address (URL) following the question to post your answer in an online forum and read others' answers. Grasping spiritual lessons at the heart-level is the whole point of studying 1 and 2 Thessalonians. Do it!

Q1. (Acts 17:1-10) Why do you think there was so much strong opposition to Paul's ministry in Thessalonica? Why do you think Paul keeps preaching the gospel, even though there is often a violent reaction against him? Does a violent reaction to our ministry necessarily mean we should stop?

http://www.joyfulheart.com/forums/index.php?showtopic=1214

Paul's Concern

Paul is now ministering in Corinth, but he is very concerned about the young church in Thessalonica that he had to leave so abruptly. They are so new to the faith, so young, under severe persecution, first from the Jews and now from the Gentiles. Will their faith survive or will they buckle under the pressure? Paul sends Timothy to Thessalonica to encourage the believers and report back how they are. Timothy has just returned with a glowing report. Paul is relieved and full of joy (3:5-6). The first part of the letter he sends back reflects his warm love for these new believers.

Salutation

First Thessalonians begins with the salutation. Different from our letters, where the addressee is mentioned first, in Greek letter-writing format the sender is mentioned first, then the recipient.

"Paul, Silas and Timothy, To the church of the Thessalonians in God the Father and the Lord Jesus Christ: Grace and peace to you." (1:1)

These three senders constitute the apostolic church-planting team that founded the church in Thessalonica.[20] It is fitting that these three address the believers there, though Paul is probably the primary author.

Short Blessing (1:1b)

After the salutation, the typical Greek letter of the time would contain a short blessing. Greeks would typically write, "Favor, grace to you!" Jews would typically begin, "Shalom, peace to you." But Paul's characteristic greeting combines the two: "Grace and peace to you" (1:1b). In 2 Thessalonians and later epistles he amplifies this a bit: "Grace to you and peace from God our Father and the Lord Jesus Christ."

By this Paul means more than either the Greek or Jewish blessing alone. While the Greeks would wish good favor to the recipient, Paul wishes God's grace, his unmerited favor by which we are saved. While the Jews would extend a wish for peace, Paul extends a wish for both grace from God and the peace with God that comes through Jesus Christ. It is a thoroughly Christian blessing.

Greek Epistolary Style

Next in Greek epistolary style of the period[21] is an introductory thanksgiving or blessing, which comprises verses 2 through 10 here. After this would come the body – the main occasion for the letter. At the end of a letter, the writer would convey some personal greetings from the family. With Paul it is usually personal greetings that link his missionary team with the recipients of the letter. The letter would conclude with a final blessing or benediction.

Constant Prayer (1:2-3)

Paul tells the Thessalonians that he is constantly praying for them.

> "[2] We always thank God for all of you, mentioning[22] you in our prayers. [3] We continually remember[23] before our God and Father your work produced by faith, your labor prompted by love, and your endurance inspired by hope in our Lord Jesus Christ." (1:2-3)

---

[20] You can learn more about Silas and Timothy in the Introduction.

[21] Peter T. O'Brien, "Letters, Letter Forms, DPL, pp. 550-553.

[22] "Mentioning" (NIV, NRSV) is actually an idiom of two words, "making mention" (KJV), *poieō*, "make, do" and *mneia*, "remembrance, memory," here, "mention" (BDAG 654, 2).

[23] The Greek noun and verb for "mention" and "remember" are the same, *mnēmoneuō*, "remember, keep in mind, think of," also—with focus on dramatic aspect of remembrance—"mention" (BDAG 655, 1a).

Whenever Paul and his team pray, they speak the names of the Thessalonians before God. Notice that Paul is praying "always"[24] (verse 2) and "continually"[25] (verse 3). His prayers for them go on day and night. Even as he is working at his trade of sewing tents he is praying. He loves these people; they are always on his heart.

God's Calling Was Very Evident (1:4-5a)

"[4] For we know, brothers loved by God, that he has chosen you, [5] because our gospel came to you not simply with words, but also with power, with the Holy Spirit and with deep conviction." (1:4-5a)

By this time in his career, Paul has spoken in scores of villages and dozens of synagogues all across Syria, Crete, Asia Minor, and Macedonia. But he recalls that when he spoke to the Thessalonians, he saw a powerful confirmation that God had chosen them. When Paul was speaking, there was a special power of the Holy Spirit that was unique. Miracles probably were evident that had a great effect on the hearers (cf. 1 Corinthians 2:4-5).

The result was deep conviction.[26] Accounts of revivals throughout the world in the last two centuries indicate the presence of this kind of deep conviction that results in repentance and faith. Without revival, so many of the conversions we see are intellectual and emotional in nature. Often they don't get to the inner person. The Thessalonian ministry was powerful and unique.

There are times when our message seems to fall on deaf ears. We try, we say the words, but there seems to be little effect. In Thessalonica it was different. There was an amazing receptivity (2:13). The power of the Spirit was unmistakable. Paul knew that God was doing something special. God had truly chosen these new disciples to establish his name in Thessalonica.

How can we have a similar result today? We need two things:

1. **Earnest, intercessory prayer.** When we realize that we can't accomplish the task of salvation, we learn how to pray and trust God. We listen for God's voice, and when we hear it, we obey. Great evangelism must be undergirded by great

---

[24] *Pantote*, "always, at all times" (BDAG 755).

[25] "Continually" (NIV), "constantly" (NRSV), "without ceasing" (KJV) is *adialeiptōs*, "constantly, unceasingly" (BDAG 20), "without intermission, incessantly ... not interrupting for a time something already begun" (Thayer, *Lexicon*, pp. 11, 139).

[26] "Conviction" (NIV, NRSV), "assurance" (KJV) is the noun *plērophoria*, "state of complete certainty, full assurance, certainty," here, "with full conviction" (BDAG 827). To emphasize the completeness of conviction, Paul modifies the noun with the adjective *polys*, "much," here with the idea of "great, strong, intense" conviction (Thayer).

prayer. The most significant people in an evangelistic campaign may not be the outward spokesmen, but the behind-the-scenes intercessors.

2. **Miracles.** Some believe that the day of miracles is over, that signs and wonders were for the apostolic age before the New Testament canon was complete. That after the New Testament was written, there was no more need for miracles. Frankly, dear friends, this is a rationalization that has no scriptural basis. Paul indicated that some would have spiritual gifts of healings, faith, and miracles (1 Corinthians 12:9-10, 29-30). So did Jesus (Mark 16:18).[27] The Book of Acts gives many indications of the power of miracles to win people to Christ. And a careful reading of church history shows many, many incidents of healing and miracles after apostolic times. To refuse to believe God for miracles in our day is rationalized unbelief! I may not have those gifts, but somewhere in our congregations, God has gifted people in this way. We need to seek out these gifted people and nurture them.

Q2. (1 Thessalonians 1:4-5) Why is the Holy Spirit's working so necessary to effective ministry? What happens when the main power behind our ministry is will-power? What is the role of miracles in Paul's evangelism? What would happen if we saw miracles in evangelism in our day? What is hindering this?
http://www.joyfulheart.com/forums/index.php?showtopic=1215

Election and Predestination (1:4)

"For we know, brothers loved by God, that he has chosen you...." (1:4)

Paul marveled that God "has chosen[28] you." There is a mystery in God's choosing or election. Why is one group receptive, but not another? The gospel is open to "whosoever" (Mark 10:32), but no one can come unless the Father draws him (John 6:44). We are

---

[27] I am aware that the earliest manuscripts don't include the "longer ending" of Mark. However, it is clear by its inclusion in most manuscripts that this was the clear expectation of the primitive church. They were seeing these signs and wonders.

[28] "Chosen" (NIV, NRSV), "election" (KJV) is *eklogē*, "a special choice, selection, choice, election," from *ek*, "out of" + *legō*, "say, speak, call" (BDAG 306, 1). In 2 Thessalonians 2:13 he refers to their choosing with a different verb, *haireō*.

called to declare the gospel to all nations (Matthew 24:14; 28:19-20; Luke 24:47), but people cannot understand the Word unless God opens their eyes to it (Luke 24:45; Acts 16:14; 26:18). I don't think it's worth grinding our mental gears somehow trying to understand predestination and election – it's beyond us. But, like Paul, our job is to listen to the Holy Spirit and then obey Him, even if it lands us in jail for witnessing of our faith.

Imitators of Paul and of the Lord (1:5b-6a)

When Paul was expelled from Thessalonica, his enemies did their best to trash his reputation. Now he hints that the Thessalonians aren't fooled by what had been said. They know his manner of life. Indeed, they had imitated him – and the Lord.

> "[5b] You know how we lived among you for your sake. [6] You became imitators[29] of us and of the Lord." (1:5b-6a)

As Paul had told the Corinthian church in 1 Corinthians 11:1:

> "**Be imitators** of me, as I am of Christ." (NRSV)
> "**Follow my example**, as I follow the example of Christ." (NIV)

It's so important that a congregation's leader or leaders are carefully imitating Christ; otherwise, the people who follow them will develop twisted characters. It's the same responsibility that parents bear to provide good examples to children who will pattern their lives after what they see in their parents.

Sometimes I hear people say that they don't need church. That they can study the Bible in the privacy of their homes. That theirs is a private faith. Hogwash! The Christian faith portrayed for us in the Bible exists in community. People who isolate themselves from the Christian community miss out on vital character formation that Christ intended: (1) Christian role models to emulate, and (2) spiritual gifts in the body to build them up and help them grow healthy. We can tell ourselves we don't need church, but that's self-deceit promoted by the devil. The Christian church is God's plan to help mature us – and to involve us in Christ's mission to our communities.

Q3. (1 Thessalonians 1:5b-6a) How important is imitation in the formation of a new Christian's spiritual life? What kinds of ministry are most conducive to imitation? Why is the character of the mentor or leader so important to the health of the church? How well do people grow in Christ who aren't part of a Christian community? In

---

[29] "Imitators" (NIV, NRSV), "followers" (KJV) is *mimētēs*, "imitator," from *mimos*, "actor," that is, one who imitates a character for a performance (BDAG 652, a; Robertson, *Word Pictures*).

1. our spiritual leader should be a good example.
2. a leader that is ~~good teacher~~ – well spoken – knows his material – a successful one –
3. we want to immitate/follow them
4. It would be very hard to grow without Church fellowship

what way is *your* character important to your family and spiritual children?

http://www.joyfulheart.com/forums/index.php?showtopic=1216

We should set good spiritual examples

Joy in the Midst of Suffering (1:6b-9a)

> "In spite of severe suffering, you welcomed the message with the joy given by the Holy Spirit. 7 And so you became a model to all the believers in Macedonia and Achaia. 8 The Lord's message rang out from you not only in Macedonia and Achaia – your faith in God has become known everywhere. Therefore we do not need to say anything about it, 9 for they themselves report what kind of reception you gave us." (1:6b-9a)

"Suffering" (NIV), "persecution" (NRSV), "affliction"(KJV) is *thlipsis*, literally, "pressing, pressure." Here it is used in a metaphorical sense, "trouble that inflicts distress, oppression, affliction, tribulation."[30] The Thessalonians were under great pressure – both at the time Paul was preaching to them as well as after Paul had been driven out of town. Yet they welcomed[31] the message with "joy given by the Holy Spirit."

Paul still marvels at their faith and brags about them to the other churches – probably at Corinth in particular, where he is writing this letter. In spite of the newness of their faith, the Thessalonians have become a "model" (NIV), "example" (NRSV), "ensample" (KJV)[32] of faith to other new believers.

It isn't just Paul bragging; others have heard of this church and passed the word. The Thessalonian church has become legendary throughout the whole area for its receptivity[33] to the gospel.

From Idols to the Living and True God (1:9b)

> "They tell how you turned to God from idols to serve the living and true God. (1:9b)

---

[30] *Thlipsis*, BDAG 457, 1.

[31] "Welcomed" (NIV), "received" (NRSV, KJV) is *dechomai*, "receive," here, "be receptive of, be open to, approve, accept" (BDAG 221, 5).

[32] The basic meaning of *typos* is "a mark made as the result of a blow or pressure." Then it becomes "copy, image." Here it refers to "an archetype serving as a model, type, pattern, model, example" (BDAG 1019-1020, 6b).

[33] "Reception" (NIV), "welcome" (NRSV), "manner of entering in" (KJV) is *eisodos*, "entrance," here figuratively, "act of finding acceptance" (BDAG 294, 3).

This is particularly remarkable to Paul, because the bulk of the converts in Thessalonica were not God-fearers, Gentiles who attended synagogue and believed the Jewish scriptures. After the initial influx of God-fearers from the synagogue (Acts 17:4), there was a powerful movement among out-and-out pagans to believe in Jesus and be baptized. The background of the majority of his readers is evident by Paul's style in this epistle. He doesn't quote the Old Testament very profusely, since he isn't arguing before Jews. Rather he explains things simply, relying upon his own authority as an apostle and upon the direct teaching of Jesus (4:15).

The Gospel in a Nutshell (1:10)

Finally, Paul remarks on the expectation of the Thessalonian believers:

> "... [10] and to wait for his Son from heaven, whom he raised from the dead – Jesus, who rescues us from the coming wrath." (1:10)

In this one verse, Paul reminds the believers of five foundational truths which are at the core of the gospel.

1. **Jesus Christ is God's Son.** It is just a reference here, no doubt, to much more thorough teaching that he had given in person when he first won them to Christ.

2. **Jesus Christ will return.** Every chapter (except one) in 1 and 2 Thessalonians has something to say about Christ's coming. It is a persistent theme of both letters (1 Thessalonians 1:10; 2:19; 3:13; 4:13-18; 5:1-4; 2 Thessalonians 1:7-10; 2:1-14).

3. **Jesus Christ has been raised from the dead.** Paul mentions this again later in the letter: "We believe that Jesus died and rose again…." (4:14).

4. **Jesus Christ is our Savior.** He has stood in our place, he took our sins upon him on the cross to rescue us from the punishment we so richly deserve.[34]

5. **God's wrath is coming upon sin.** Our age has rejected the idea of accountability to God – and even of the reality of sin. They don't believe in the wrath of God against sin – or at least they suppress that thought most of the time. That certain

---

[34] "Rescues" (NIV, NRSV), "delivered" (KJV) is *rhyomai*, "to rescue from danger, save, rescue, deliver, preserve someone" (BDAG 907-908). Here Paul uses the word in a spiritual sense, to save a person from eternal death. However, the word is used most often of rescue from temporal perils. Much more common for spiritual salvation is the verb *sōzō*, "save" (2:10, 16), the noun *sōtēria*, "salvation" (5:8-9; 2 Thessalonians 2:13), and the noun *sōtēr*, "Savior."

and terrible judgment is another theme of these letters (1 Thessalonians 2:16; 5:9; 2 Thessalonians 1:5, 7-8; 2:12).

Q4. (1 Thessalonians 1:10) What does verse 10 teach us about the Christian faith? Which of these elements are most important? Which are less important? Which are underemphasized by the church in our day?

http://www.joyfulheart.com/forums/index.php?showtopic=1217

we have faith that Jesus will return
all are equally important.
underemphasized — the wrath of God is coming

Signs that God has chosen you (1:4-10)

We can summarize the first chapter of this letter by enumerating the signs that God has chosen the Thessalonians – the secret of them being bountiful believers:

1. They received the gospel, which was presented with spiritual power and miraculous manifestations.

2. They imitated Paul and welcomed his message.

3. They exhibited joy in the face of persecution.

4. They became a model to other believers.

5. They turned from idols to the true and living God.

6. They have an expectation of Christ's coming.

Dear friend, if you were to examine your own life and its fruits, what would be the signs that God has chosen you? I don't ask this to put you on the spot, but to help you reflect on the fruit of God's working in your own life. You might find two or three manifestations, but probably will be able to list one or two dozen indications if you think about it. Thanks be to God for his gracious work in us who believe in Him.

Prayer

Father, we praise you for your powerful work in bringing unbelievers to Christ. We long to see your powerful conviction touch our relatives and friends, our neighbors and cities. O Lord, send revival among us that "sinners be converted and your name glorified." [35] In Jesus' name, we pray. Amen.

---

[35] This phrase is from the hymn "Pentecostal Power," by Charles H. Gabriel (1912).

Key Verse

"They tell how you turned to God from idols to serve the living and true God, and to wait for his Son from heaven, whom he raised from the dead – Jesus, who rescues us from the coming wrath." (1 Thessalonians 1:9b-10)

2. The Character of a Disciple-Maker
(1 Thessalonians 2:1-16)

If you've ever been falsely criticized you know how hard it is to bear. How personally devastated you feel. And you're concerned that people will actually believe the lies. When Paul and his team were driven out of Thessalonica after only months of ministry, they were hammered with dozens of scurrilous allegations.

The Jews who had rejected Paul's teaching had stirred up the mob to a frenzy. The crowd went *en masse* to get Paul. When they couldn't find him, they took Jason, a Jew who had embraced the Christian message, and hauled him and other believers before the civil authorities. A riot was in the offing. Completely false charges were made to discredit Paul and the fledgling church. It was a very difficult time.

Our Mission Was Not a Failure (2:1)

As soon as he could, Paul wrote this letter to reassure the Thessalonian believers and help put into perspective what had happened – to set the record straight regarding his own character. But he also understood the need to ground these new Christians – most of them fresh from paganism – in Christian character themselves. He writes,

> "You know, brothers, that our visit to you was not a failure." (2:1)

Paul begins with an evaluation of the success of his mission. To the Thessalonians it may have seemed cut short, aborted, a failure. Paul insists that his mission was not in vain.[36] He had come to preach Christ and establish a Christian congregation in the city – and had succeeded, even though his part in it had been cut short by vicious persecution.

Jesus' last words to his disciples, recorded at the end of Matthew's gospel, outline the centrality of Jesus' mission to make disciples:

> "All authority in heaven and on earth has been given to me. Therefore go and make disciples of all nations, baptizing them in the name of the Father and of the Son and of the Holy Spirit, and teaching them to obey everything I have commanded you. And surely I am with you always, to the very end of the age." (Matthew 28:18-20)

---

[36] "Failure" (NIV), "in vain" (NRSV, KJV) is two words, "not" and *kenos*, "empty," here, "pertaining to being without purpose or result, in vain" (BDAG 539, 3).

Paul had made disciples in Thessalonica. The mission was a success, in so far that he followed the "Prime Directive."

Courage to Take Risks for the Gospel (2:2)

Paul's first task is to help the Thessalonians understand that making disciples must often take place among risks. That's the nature of this spiritual warfare.

> "We had previously suffered[37] and been insulted[38] in Philippi, as you know, but with the help of our God we dared to tell you his gospel in spite of strong opposition.[39]" (2:2)

I was beat up and imprisoned in Philippi, Paul reminds them, but that didn't stop me from declaring the gospel to you. The first character trait that he hopes them to comprehend – and emulate – is courage to speak the gospel, even if people oppose them. "We *dared* to tell you his gospel," Paul says. "Dared" (NIV), "had courage" (NRSV), "were bold" (KJV) is *parrēsiazomai*, "speak freely, openly, fearlessly." Here it has the sense, "have the courage, venture."[40] Christian courage and boldness is vital to the success of Christ's kingdom.

Jesus told his disciples many times that preaching the gospel is dangerous – but necessary.

> "Because of the increase of wickedness, the love of most will grow cold, but he who stands firm to the end will be saved. And this gospel of the kingdom will be preached in the whole world as a testimony to all nations, and then the end will come." (Matthew 24:12-14)

In our day, many, many believers have been effectively silenced by the "opposition." We're afraid to offend, not wanting to be ostracized from polite society. And so we lack courage and boldness. We are unable to take the risks necessary to propagate the Christian faith, and so the number of new believers dwindles over time.

Courage in the face of opposition is one of the first character traits of effective disciple-makers.

Q1. (1 Thessalonians 2:2) Why is personal courage such an important character trait for a disciple – and for a discipler? How does lack of courage prevent evangelism?

no one would listen to the message of a wimpy person one who is afraid – dosint speek out.

[37] "Previously suffered" (NIV) is *propaschō*, "suffer previously" (BDAG 873).

[38] "Insulted" (NIV), "shamefully (en)treated" (NRSV, KJV) is *hybrizō*, "to treat in an insolent or spiteful manner, mistreat, scoff at, insult" (BDAG 1022).

[39] "Opposition" (NIV, NRSV), "contention" (KJV) is *agōn*, "a struggle against opposition, struggle, fight" (BDAG 17, 2).

[40] *Parrēsiazomai*, BDAG 782, 2.

How does lack of courage prevent a congregation from being healthy? What is God calling you to do that will require courage on your part?
http://www.joyfulheart.com/forums/index.php?showtopic=1218

No Courage in a Congregation — no growth to be a witness for him — how to do it?

An Appeal from Honest Motives (2:3-6)

Why does Paul use good parchment to talk about his motives? I can think of two reasons:

1. **To restore his reputation**. Paul's reputation had been attacked, as I discussed above.

2. **To highlight appropriate motives for the believers**. It's easy for us humans to become corrupted and turned from pure motives to self-seeking ones. Paul is trying to help his disciples become more self-aware, to correct tendencies that may be lurking within them that are less than honorable.

So Paul examines sincerity and honesty.

> "³ For the appeal we make does not spring from error or impure motives, nor are we trying to trick you. ⁴ On the contrary, we speak as men approved by God to be entrusted with the gospel. We are not trying to please men but God, who tests our hearts. ⁵ You know we never used flattery, nor did we put on a mask to cover up greed – God is our witness. ⁶ We were not looking for praise from men, not from you or anyone else." (2:3-6)

Paul considers the various motives that sometimes drive people who advocate a cause,[41] and one by one discards them regarding himself and his gospel team.

1. **Misguided belief**. "Error" (NIV), "deceit" (NRSV, KJV) is *planē*, "wandering from the path of truth, error, delusion, deceit, deception."[42] The English word "planet" comes from this word, since planets used to be considered as "wandering stars." Sometimes people get some harebrained idea that is off the track, and then try to persuade everyone else that this misguided doctrine is correct.

---

[41] "Appeal" (NIV, NRSV), "exhortation" (KJV) is *paraklēsis*, "act of emboldening another in belief or course of action, encouragement, exhortation" (BDAG 760, 1).
[42] *Planē*, BDAG 822.

2. **Impure motives,**[43] sometimes as a way to seduce women. Sometimes the desire for money, sex, or power lie behind a person's advocacy. It's important to examine and know ourselves, so we can find freedom from motives that drive us that may be hidden from even us.

3. **Trickery, intentional deceit.**[44] Some pastors, I am sorry to say, and some televangelists, use gimmicks and tricks to manipulate their followers. Christ requires openness and honesty of us.

4. **Men-pleasers,** telling people what they want to hear. If Christian workers act like politicians, then they deserve the level of trust that politicians have earned for themselves.

5. **Flattery,**[45] appealing to people's vanity. Some people are very skilled at manipulating people by massaging the ego. We need to be aware of people's vanity, but be careful not to stoop to manipulation rather than true disciple-making.

6. **Greed,**[46] exploiting religion in order to gain wealth. Sadly, many outside the church believe that "all the church wants is money" – and sometimes their assessment is correct. We must make sure that greed doesn't drive us.

7. **Reputation or fame.**[47] Many is the preacher and Christian worker who needs the approval of people to feel good about himself or herself. Thus approval and acclaim is courted and sought. Decisions are made on the basis of how people will respond. It can be a serious weakness. Pride and personal career advancement get in the way of doing the work of the Lord for its own sake.

Christian workers are not immune from character flaws. But having examined the common character flaws – things he has surely been accused of – Paul tells the Thessalonians that he has been tested and approved[48] by God. He explains that bearing

---

[43] "Impure motives" (NIV, NRSV), "uncleanness" (KJV) is *akatharsia*, "uncleanness," here, "a state of moral corruption, immorality, vileness" (BDAG 34, 2).

[44] "Trickery" (NRSV, cf. NIV), "guile" (KJV) is *dolos*, "taking advantage through craft and underhanded methods, deceit, cunning, treachery" (BDAG 250).

[45] "Flattery" (NIV), "flattering words" (NRSV, KJV) is *kolakeia*, "flattery," from a derivative of *kolax* (a fawner) (BDAG 555).

[46] "Greed" (NIV, NRSV), "covetousness" (KJV) is *pleonexia*, "the state of desiring to have more than one's due, greediness, insatiableness, avarice, covetousness" (BDAG 824).

[47] "Praise" (NIV, NRSV), "glory" (KJV) is *doxa*, "glory," here, "honor as enhancement or recognition of status or performance, fame, recognition, renown, honor, prestige" (BDAG 257, 3).

[48] "Approved" (NIV, NRSV), "allowed" (KJV) is *dokimazō*, "to draw a conclusion about worth on the basis of testing, prove, approve," here, "accept as proved, approve ... found worthy" (BDAG 256, 2b).

the message of the gospel is a sacred trust,[49] not some means of advancing his own agenda. Too often professional Christian leaders get confused. They may begin by wanting to serve God and do his will, but later on they come to see ministry as a job, a profession, and a way of earning a living, enjoying status, and exercising power. They have become corrupted. It's an all-too-common tale. Dear friend, what are your motives for ministry – really? Deep down?

For example, let's look at the motivations that drive believers to tell others about Jesus.

1. **Love**, actual deep concern for their lives and futures. Hopefully! But often, motives are mixed. Sometimes Christians witness out of:

2. **Guilt and duty**. They feel bad that they haven't shared their faith, and are "grinding it out" because it makes them feel better about themselves.

3. **Pride**. Sometimes Christians like to brag about how many people they have won to Christ, as if they are displaying scalps as trophies of their spiritual prowess.

4. **Self-righteousness.** I've heard believers "witness" by condemning people for their sins (rightly being perceived as "holier than thou"), rather than pointing to what Jesus has done for them. There can be a certain perverse pleasure in telling people they're going to hell – especially if you don't really love them! What it comes down to is pride – I'm better than you!

Dear friends, our hidden motives have a lot to do with the quality of our ministry for Christ. We need to grow up in Christ, rather than remain children! And Paul was trying to raise a crop of healthy disciples. That's what this letter is about.

Q2. (1 Thessalonians 2:3-6) Which of the character flaws mentioned in these verses is the greatest problem in the church? Why do you say that? How can you prevent one of these character flaws from overtaking you?

http://www.joyfulheart.com/forums/index.php?showtopic=1219

Probably – saying what someone wants to hear
I've done it.
Think – think think then talk.

---

[49] "Entrusted" (NIV, NRSV), "put in trust" (KJV) is *pisteuō*, "believe," here transitive, "entrust something to someone" (BDAG 818, 3).

Refusal to Impose a Financial Burden (2:6b, 9)

Paul is still trying to help the believers understand the purity of his motives – that he took no financial help from them at all (as he spells out in verse 9).

> "As apostles of Christ we could have been a burden to you...." (2:6b)
> "Surely you remember, brothers, our toil and hardship; we worked night and day in
> order not to be a burden to anyone while we preached the gospel of God to you." (2:9)

As in his ministry to the Corinthians, later on this Second Missionary Journey, Paul asserts his right as an apostle[50] to receive support from the believers. But then he specifically renounces that privilege so that he wouldn't impose a financial burden[51] on them.

> "4 Don't we have the right to food and drink? 5 Don't we have the right to take a believ-
> ing wife along with us, as do the other apostles and the Lord's brothers and Cephas? ...
> 12b But we did not use this right.... 18 What then is my reward? Just this: that in preaching
> the gospel I may offer it free of charge, and so not make use of my rights in preaching
> it." (1 Corinthians 9:4-5, 12b, 18)

It's important – especially in Thessalonica – that he explain his policy of earning his own keep (probably as a tent-maker as in Corinth, Acts 18:2-3), because, as we'll see, there were some in the church who were free-loading off of the others. Later in the letter, he instructs them:

> "Make it your ambition to lead a quiet life, to mind your own business and to work with
> your hands, just as we told you, so that your daily life may win the respect of outsiders
> and so that you will not be dependent on anybody." (4:11-12)

But they didn't seem to get it. So in 2 Thessalonians 3:6-15 he is very clear and direct that any freeloading must stop.

Paul's example of working a secular job while preaching the gospel is relevant to our own day, when many pastors, perhaps most – looking at it from a worldwide perspec-tive – are "bi-vocational." They earn their living in a secular job and then preach the gospel because God has called them to it. Our phrase "full-time Christian service" presupposes Western wealth, and does not represent Bible teaching. Of course, if a church is able to support a pastor, that is a wonderful thing – it helps the congregation

---

[50] "Apostles" is the plural of the Greek noun *apostolos*, which probably originally means "sending out." Here it refers to "a messenger with extraordinary status, especially of God's messenger, envoy, delegate, ambassador" (BDAG 122, 2c).
[51] "Be a burden" (NIV), "made demands" (NRSV), "be burdensome" (KJV) is two words, *en*, "with," and *baros*, "weight, burden," here figuratively, perhaps "experience of something that is particularly oppressive, burden" (BDAG 167, 2).

and enables the leader to put more time into the work. Don't stop paying your pastor! But for Paul it was a hindrance in missionary work, with the "burden"[52] it imposed on the new flock.

Since the Thessalonian church had a problem with some overly-dependent members, Paul teaches them by his own example of self-sufficiency. To work is a godly and good thing. Notice the words that Paul uses to describe his secular work:

> "Surely you remember, brothers, our toil and hardship; we worked night and day...." (2:9a)

He emphasizes the tiresome, grueling aspect of work – then glories in it! We'll consider this further in Lesson 9, where this phrase is repeated nearly word-for-word in 2 Thessalonians 3:8.

Like a Mother Caring for Her Children (2:6b-8)

Rather than expecting his spiritual children to support their parent, Paul pours out himself for them.

> "[6b] As apostles of Christ we could have been a burden to you, [7] but we were gentle among you, like a mother caring for her little children. [8] We loved you so much that we were delighted to share with you not only the gospel of God but our lives as well, because you had become so dear to us." (2:6b-8)

I look at the qualities mentioned in this chapter as qualities of a disciple-maker, who doesn't seek to further his own interests, but the interests of those to whom God sends him or her. You may have a ministry as one of those disciple-makers – to one or two individuals, or even to a whole congregation.

Paul talks about the nurturing qualities that are especially found in mothers.[53]

1. **Gentleness.** The Greek word "gentle" is *ēpios*. It has the root idea of "affable," then, "mild, gentle."[54] When it's used of persons it has the idea of "gentle, kind," as well as "soothing, assuaging."[55]

2. **Caring.** "Caring" (NIV), "tenderly caring" (NRSV), "cherisheth" (KJV) is *thalpō*. In Greek literature often in the sense, "make warm." Here it is figurative: "cherish, comfort."[56]

---

[52] "Be a burden" (NIV, NRSV), "be chargeable" (KJV) is *epibareō*, "to be a burden to, weigh down, burden" (BDAG 368).

[53] "Mother" (NIV), "nurse" (NRSV, KJV) is *trophos*, "nurse," possibly, "mother" (BDAG 1017).

[54] *Ēpios*, Thayer, 279.

[55] *Ēpios*, Liddell-Scott.

[56] *Thalpō*, BDAG 442.

3. **Sharing one's life**. In our day, ministers are sometimes taught to keep a "professional distance" from parishioners. Don't get too close, they are warned. Of course, there are dangers and vulnerabilities in getting close. But Paul reminds the Thessalonians of his own ministry style – "sharing[57] ... our own lives" (2:8b). Disciples are not best made through arms-length teaching, but by sharing life-to-life. That's how Jesus did it, and so did Paul. And that's how mothers raise their sons and daughters.

Q3. (1 Thessalonians 2:6b-8) Why are "motherly" nurturing qualities so important to growing disciples? How effectively can male disciplers adopt some of these traits?
http://www.joyfulheart.com/forums/index.php?showtopic=1220

a new child in Christ need to be guided + nurtured a parent guides wether female or male.

A Holy and Blameless Life (2:10)

In contrast to accusations they have heard, Paul asks the Thessalonians to consider what they have seen in his conduct and lifestyle.

"You are witnesses, and so is God, of how holy, righteous and blameless we were among you who believed." (2:10)

1. **"Holy" or "pure"**[58] means that we live lives that will be pleasing to God. If we're making disciples – or raising children – they'll surely see the inconsistencies in us if we're not seeking to do this. "Do as I say, not as I do," does not work!

2. **"Righteous"**[59] is similar, but it emphasizes our uprightness according to God's standard.

3. **"Blameless"**[60] suggests that we give no one any just cause to accuse us.

---

[57] "Sharing" (NIV, NRSV), "to have imparted" (KJV) is *metadidōmi*, "to give (a part of), impart, share" (BDAG 638). This compound verb comes from *meta-*, "association, fellowship, participation with" + *didōmi*, "to give." (Thayer, *meta-*, III,1).

[58] "Holy" (NIV), "pure" (NRSV), "holily" (KJV) is *hosiōs*, "pertaining to a manner pleasing to God, devoutly." Used only here in the New Testament (BDAG 728).

[59] "Righteous" (NIV), "upright" (NRSV), "justly" (KJV) is *dikaiōs*, is from the realm of law, "just or right in a juridical sense." Here it pertains to quality of character, thought, or behavior, "correctly, justly, uprightly" (BDAG 256, 2).

Isn't this an impossibly high standard for a disciple-maker? After all, "We're not perfect," we mutter as a kind of excuse. But this is *Christ's* standard. We are *his* men and women, not our own. "We have been bought with a price!" (1 Corinthians 6:20).

Of course, we'll sin now and again. The difference is that we are sincerely seeking for our lives to be pleasing to God, not just mouthing the words. In a job setting, a worker who strives to do a difficult task accurately may make some mistakes as he or she is learning, but eventually the job becomes second nature. Yes, there are occasional mistakes. But the mistakes don't characterize the performance. That's the way we should look at sin. Not as defeated Christians, but as Christians who believe in Christ's victory over our lives.

When we do sin – before our disciples or before our children – then we acknowledge the sin (confess) and ask forgiveness of those we have sinned against or disappointed. If we just bluster on through as if we had never sinned, people will see us as hypocrites. If we are honest and transparent about it, people will see us as sincere, but imperfect, servants of Christ. And that will be enough to be effective disciple-makers.

As a Father with His Children (2:11-12)

Paul has explored some of the nurturing qualities often associated with mothers. Now he moves to some of the qualities commonly associated with fathers.

> "[11] For you know that we dealt with[61] each of you as a father deals with his own children, [12] encouraging, comforting and urging you to live lives worthy of God, who calls you into his kingdom and glory." (2:11-12)

Good fathers help their children strive to be the very best they can be. They accomplish this in several ways:

1. **Exhorting**. The word Paul uses here, *parakaleō*, can carry a variety of nuances, depending upon the context – "to urge strongly, appeal to, urge, exhort, encourage."[62] With the other words in this sentence it probably carries the idea of "to exhort or urge." Whatever the exact sense here, it pictures a father who is actively engaged in molding his children's lives.

---

[60] "Blameless" (NIV, NRSV), "unblameably" (KJV) is *amemptos*, used especially in the Greco-Roman world of people of extraordinary civic consciousness, "blamelessly," so there is no cause for censure (BDAG 52; Thayer, 32), literally, "without blame."

[61] "Dealt with" (NIV, NRSV) is added to make the sentence smoother in English. It isn't in the Greek text, though is implied.

[62] *Parakaleō*, BDAG 765, 2.

2. **Encouraging or comforting** is *paramytheomai*, "console, cheer up someone," especially in connection with death or other tragic events.[63] If exhorting is a more forceful word, then encouraging or comforting is the other side. I can imagine a father (or mother) putting his arms around a small child who is hurt and confused, and comforting him or her.

3. **Urging or pleading.** The third word is *martyromai*, "bear witness," here with the sense, "to urge something as a matter of great importance, affirm, insist, implore."[64] It has the idea of to speak with all seriousness and urgency to a child.

The purpose of these disciple-making behaviors is to mold men and women into consistent followers of Jesus Christ, so that they live lives[65] that are worthy or suitable[66] to God's own kingdom and glory – a high calling indeed.

The NIV leaves out an important word in verse 12 – "own" – which is included in the Greek text and is important to the sense. You are called to God's *own* kingdom and glory. It is a privilege. It is incumbent upon you to conform to God's standards, not to your own or to those of the world. Your lives need to reflect *his* value system. We are called to a much higher standard than our neighbors – God's *own* character and holiness.

Q4. (1 Thessalonians 2:11-12) Why are "fatherly" roles so important to making disciples? How effectively do you think women can adopt these traits?
http://www.joyfulheart.com/forums/index.php?showtopic=1221

a father leads – guides – encourages + sets an example for his children
100%

Receptivity to God's Word (2:13a)

Paul was amazed at the Thessalonians' incredible receptivity (which we discussed in Lesson 1, at 1:4-5a).

> "And we also thank God continually because, when you received[67] the word of God, which you heard from us, you accepted it not as the word of men, but as it actually is, the word of God, which is at work in you who believe." (2:13)

---

[63] *Paramytheomai*, BDAG 769.
[64] *Martyromai*, BDAG 619, 2.
[65] "To live lives" (NIV), "lead a life" (NRSV), "walk" (KJV) is *peripateō*, "walk," here, figuratively, "to conduct one's life, comport oneself, behave, live as habit of conduct" (BDAG 803, 2aα).
[66] "Worthy" is *axiōs*, "worthily, in a manner worthy of, suitably" (BDAG 94).

Paul had seen a lot of rejection of the gospel in his ministry. So have we. Unbelievers perceive the gospel and the Bible as a man-made religion, not as the actual "word of God" – or they would respond to it differently. The Thessalonians, to their great credit, took Paul's words as the "gospel truth," and so were saved.

To see this degree of receptivity takes an act of God. C. Peter Wagner recalls the city of Resistencia in northern Argentina that was resistant to the revival that was sweeping Argentina at that time. Of the 400,000 population, fewer than 6,000 were evangelical believers. But receptivity came when the believers were taught intercessory prayer, what Wager calls "strategic-level spiritual warfare." The evangelical population grew to 100,000.[68] Dear friends, if we want a revival characterized by great receptivity among unbelievers, we must learn to pray that the demonic forces that blind them (2 Corinthians 4:4) will be defeated.

The Effective, Working Word of God (2:13b)

Look at verse 13 one more time:

> "... You received the word of God, which you heard from us ... the word of God, which is at work in you who believe." (2:13)

Notice that the Word, once received, "is at work[69] in you who believe." Like yeast in dough, it is changing and transforming the dough over time. The word doesn't just mean to *work*, but to *work and product an effect*, which the KJV brings out in its translation, "effectually worketh." Consider the power of God's word in these verses:

> "You are already **clean** because of the word I have spoken to you." (John 15:3)

> "**Sanctify** them by the truth; your word is truth." (John 17:17)

---

[67] "Received" is *paralambanō*, "to gain control of or receive jurisdiction over, take over, receive," here referring to receiving and accepting a spiritual heritage (BDAG 768, 2bγ). "To receive something transmitted" with the mind (Thayer, 484, 2b). This compound has such senses as "to take over," for example, to take over an intellectual position, and "to inherit," especially intellectual things, such as a student from a teacher. "It is important in philosophy, for most knowledge is handed down orally, and since it is practical, the teacher is an authoritative leader whose goal is the formation of character and who will still be respected even should the students strike out on their own (cf. Socrates)" (Gerhard Delling, *lambanō, ktl.*, TDNT 4:5-15).

[68] Discussed several of Wagner's books, including C. Peter Wagner, *Wrestling with Alligators, Prophets, and Theologians* (Regal, 2010), pp. 180-182.

[69] "Is at work" (NIV, NRSV), "effectually worketh" (KJV) is *energeō*, "to put one's capabilities into operation, work, be at work, be active, operate, be effective," (here, in the middle voice with an impersonal subject) (BDAG 335, 1b). Milligan sees the word as passive, meaning here "to set in operation" (cited in Robertson, *Word Pictures*).

"But thanks be to God that, though you used to be slaves to sin, you wholeheartedly obeyed the form of teaching to which you were entrusted. You have been **set free from sin** and have become slaves to righteousness." (Romans 6:17-18)

"Faith comes from hearing the message, and the message is heard through the word of Christ." (Romans 10:17)

"... The word of truth, the gospel.... All over the world this gospel is **bearing fruit and growing**." (Colossians 1:5b-6a)

"Our gospel came to you not simply with words, but also **with power**, with the Holy Spirit and with **deep conviction**." (1 Thessalonians 1:5) •

"For the word of God is **living and active. Sharper** than any double-edged sword, it penetrates even to dividing soul and spirit, joints and marrow; it **judges** the thoughts and attitudes of the heart." (Hebrews 4:12)

"He chose to **give us birth** through the word of truth, that we might be a kind of firstfruits of all he created." (James 1:18)

"You have been **born again**, not of perishable seed, but of imperishable, through the living and enduring word of God." (1 Peter 1:23)

Because of the power of God's word, the role of teacher in a congregation is a very powerful agent for change, growth, and discipleship.

Q5. (1 Thessalonians 2:13) What is the role of the Word of God in molding disciples' lives? Does it have a power of its own? How does that seem to operate? What are the implications for disciplers of this powerful action of the Word?

http://www.joyfulheart.com/forums/index.php?showtopic=1222

We study the Word & try to live as Christ would have us to live.

YES!

It leads & guides us

Because of it – lives can be changed.

Persecution from Countrymen (2:14-16)

Paul concludes this section on character with a sad commentary on the character of the Thessalonian church's opponents.

It seems that the Thessalonians' primary enemies weren't the Jews at all, but their own countrymen, who persecuted them, probably because they neglected the local deities and worshipped what was perceived to be a foreign deity. Paul compares the persecution the Thessalonians were experiencing to the persecution being suffered by the believers in Judea – except that in Judea the enemies were their Jewish countrymen.

"¹⁴ For you, brothers, became imitators of God's churches in Judea, which are in Christ Jesus: You suffered from your own countrymen the same things those churches suffered from the Jews, ¹⁵ who killed the Lord Jesus and the prophets and also drove us out. They displease God and are hostile to all men ¹⁶ in their effort to keep us from speaking to the Gentiles so that they may be saved. In this way they always heap up their sins to the limit. The wrath of God has come upon them at last." (2:14-16)

You must understand! Paul, the Jew, is not anti-Semitic. To the Romans he wrote:

"I have great sorrow and unceasing anguish in my heart. For I could wish that I myself were cursed and cut off from Christ for the sake of my brothers, those of my own race, the people of Israel." (Romans 9:2-4a)

"Brothers, my heart's desire and prayer to God for the Israelites is that they may be saved." (Romans 10:1)

But Paul is angry that his fellow Jews have placed themselves in opposition first to Jesus, and then to prevent the propagation of the gospel that is able to save all who believe. Those who prevent people from hearing the gospel incur tremendous guilt. Jesus spoke a similar indictment on Jewish religious leaders:

"Woe to you experts in the law, because you have taken away the key to knowledge. You yourselves have not entered, and you have hindered those who were entering." (Luke 11:52)

Notice how important preaching the gospel is in our passage:

"[The Jews] keep us from speaking to the Gentiles so that they may be saved" (2:16a).

The Word of God, the preaching of the gospel is essential for salvation. To the Romans, Paul wrote:

"How, then, can they call on the one they have not believed in? And how can they believe in the one of whom they have not heard? And how can they hear without someone preaching to them? And how can they preach unless they are sent? As it is written, 'How beautiful are the feet of those who bring good news!'" (Romans 10:14-15)

How very selfish we are if we have grown tired of preaching the gospel to the lost – whether in our own community, or homeland, or abroad. Christianity is at its root a "pass it on" faith that cannot be stifled. When we neglect evangelism, we both displease God and show our lack of love for those who need salvation.

In this lesson we've examined the importance of character for the apostle and disciple-maker. Character is essential for credibility of the discipler. It is also essential so that the new disciples can model their own character on a life that is solid in Christ.

Friend, how is your character? What are your character flaws? I encourage you to bring them to Christ. You might also ask a Christian you trust to pray with you about these character flaws, so that prayer and accountability might help you mature in Christ. You can't be a good representative of Christ in your world or be an effective discipler unless Christ grows his character in you. Give yourself to this work of the Spirit!

Prayer

Father, we fall so short sometimes. And then we excuse our sins and weaknesses, rather than allowing you to change us. Forgive us, we pray. Work in us. Cleanse us of our sins, and make us strong in you, that we might be servants of whom you are proud. In Jesus' name, we pray. Amen.

Key Verses

"We speak as men approved by God to be entrusted with the gospel. We are not trying to please men but God, who tests our hearts." (1 Thessalonians 2:4)

"We were gentle among you, like a mother caring for her little children." (1 Thessalonians 2:7)

"We loved you so much that we were delighted to share with you not only the gospel of God but our lives as well, because you had become so dear to us." (1 Thessalonians 2:8)

"We also thank God continually because, when you received the word of God, which you heard from us, you accepted it not as the word of men, but as it actually is, the word of God, which is at work in you who believe." (1 Thessalonians 2:13)

3. The Warm Heart of a Disciple-Maker
(1 Thessalonians 2:17-3:13)

In Lesson 2 we examined the character of a disciple-maker. In this lesson we'll examine the emotions of Paul, the disciple-maker. And we'll also discuss the rewards – in addition to salvation – that come to believers at Christ's return.

Paul Longs to See Them Again (2:17-18)

As you may recall, Paul's mission to Thessalonica was abruptly cut short when the Jews fomented a riot and then blamed Paul and his followers for causing trouble, resulting in their expulsion from the city.

> "[17] Brothers, when we were torn away from you for a short time (in person, not in thought), out of our intense longing we made every effort to see you. [18] For we wanted to come to you – certainly I, Paul, did, again and again – but Satan stopped us." (2:17-18)

You can feel Paul's heart in these verses. When he was forced to leave the city it difficult for the new church, but it was wrenching for Paul himself. He describes it as being "torn away from you" (NIV). The word Paul uses (*aporphanizo*) introduces the image a sudden separation of parent and child. The word can refer either to children deprived of their parents or to parents deprived of their children. Here it refers to bereavement in general The emphasis is on unnatural separation, both forcible and painful.[70]

Paul mentions his emotion of "intense longing"[71] to see them. Paul feels the separation acutely, even though it has been only a short time – probably just a few months at most.

---

[70] Stott, *1 and 2 Thessalonians*, pp. 61-62, citing Ernest Best, *A Commentary on the First and Second Epistles to the Thessalonians* (Black's New Testament Commentary; A. & C. Black, 1972), p. 124. The word *aporphanizo* (we get our English word "orphan" from the same root – *orphanizō*), can have two meanings: "to make an orphan of someone" (BDAG 119) and "to bereave of a parent or parents" (Thayer, p. 57, from *apo*, "from" + "*orphanizō*, "make orphan").

[71] "Intense longing" (NIV), "great eagerness" (NRSV), "great desire" (KJV) translate a combination of two words, the comparative adjective *polys*, "much" and *epithymia*, "a great desire for something, desire, longing, craving" (BDAG 372, 1b). Later in 3:6, we see the same idea expressed by the verb *epipotheō*.

Prevented by Satan from Returning to Thessalonica (2:18)

He longs to see them and has tried several times to do just that, "But Satan stopped[72] us..." (2:18b). What was the Satanic hindrance that kept Paul from returning to Thessalonica? There have been several speculations:

1. Jewish opposition, perhaps a plot formed against him by the Jews.

2. His "thorn in the flesh," a bodily ailment (2 Corinthians 12:7; Galatians 4:13-14).

3. The legal ban the city leaders put on Jason (Acts 17:19), with severe penalties if Paul were to return.

4. A sin or scandal that detained him in Corinth.

The truth is, we just don't know exactly what that Satanic hindrance was.

Paul had been "hindered" elsewhere in his ministry. Prior to landing in Macedonia, Paul and his missionary team are "kept[73] by the Holy Spirit from preaching the word in the province of Asia," (Acts 16:6), and then not "allowed"[74] by the Spirit of Jesus to enter Bithynia and evangelize there (Acts 16:7). God had a mission for them in Macedonia, finally revealed in a dream where Paul saw "a man from Macedonia" calling them to come (Acts 16:9-10).

After writing these letters to the Thessalonians, Paul is prevented[75] (Romans 1:13) and often hindered[76] (Romans 15:22) from travelling to Rome. Here we're not told whether God or Satan did the hindering.

Sometimes Paul is hindered by Satan (2:18c); at other times by the Holy Spirit (Acts 16:7). How does Paul know the hindrance from travelling to Thessalonica is Satan, rather than God who is greater? Probably his discernment of the spiritual dynamics of the situation. Ultimately, of course, God works out his purpose in spite of Satan's obstacles. Whatever the case, Paul's purpose in our letter to explain to his beloved children in the faith that he couldn't return due to circumstances beyond his control, even though he desperately longed to see them. Perhaps his enemies had told the believers that Paul didn't care about them or he would have returned.

---

[72] "Stopped" (NIV), "blocked our way" (NRSV), "hindered" (KJV) is *enkoptō*, literally, "to cut into," then figuratively, "to make progress slow or difficult, hinder, thwart" (BDAG 274), from *en*, "in, into" + *koptō*, "cut, smite, strike."

[73] "Prevented" (NIV, NRSV), "let" (KJV) is *kōlyō*, "to keep something from happening, hinder, prevent, forbid" (BDAG 586, 1a).

[74] "Allow" (NIV, NRSV), "suffer" (KJV) is *eaō*, "to allow someone to do something, let, permit" (BDAG 269, 1).

[75] *Kōlyō*.

[76] Passive of *enkoptō*.

You Are Our Hope, Our Joy, Our Crown (2:19-20)

> "[19] For what is our hope, our joy, or the crown in which we will glory in the presence of our Lord Jesus when he comes? Is it not you? [20] Indeed, you are our glory[77] and joy." (2:19-20)

When we think of "crown," we think of a king's crown. But the word Paul uses indicates a laurel wreath that was awarded to the winning runner or athlete in the games.[78] Paul uses this image in 1 Corinthians:

> "Everyone who competes in the games goes into strict training. They do it to get a crown that will not last; but we do it to get a crown that will last forever." (1 Corinthians 9:25)

Paul's converts are his "crown" or prize, the evidence that he has not "run in vain" (Galatians 2:2). He calls the Philippian believers, "my joy and my crown" (Philippians 4:1). These converts in Thessalonica will be the basis of his glorying "in the presence of our Lord Jesus when he comes." This "crown" will be Paul's "glory" (NIV), "crown of boasting" (NRSV), "crown of rejoicing" (KJV), *kauchēsis*, "act of taking pride in something, boasting," or perhaps, "that which constitutes a source of pride, object of boasting, reason for boasting."[79]

In other words, Paul will present his converts to Christ at his return as the proof of his labor, as he says elsewhere,

> "...That I may boast (*kauchēma*[80]) on the day of Christ that I did not run or labor for nothing." (Philippians 2:16).

> "We will boast (*kauchēma*) of you in the day of the Lord Jesus." (2 Corinthians 1:14)

Rewards on the Day of the Lord for Service

This all sounds very much like Jesus' Parable of the Talents (Matthew 25:14-30) and Parable of the Pounds or Minas (Luke 19:12-27), where the returning master calls in each of his servants, has them present what they've accomplished, and rewards them appropriately.

---

[77] The word here is *doxa*, "glory," in this context, "honor as enhancement or recognition of status or performance, fame, recognition, renown, honor, prestige" (BDAG 257, 3).

[78] The word is *stephanos*, "a wreath made of foliage or designed to resemble foliage and worn by one of high status or held in high regard, wreath, crown." Here it is used figuratively, "that which serves as adornment or source of pride, adornment, pride" (BDAG 944, 2).

[79] *Kauchēsis*, BDAG 537, 1 and 2.

[80] *Kauchēma* is a synonym of *kauchēsis*, and means the "act of taking pride in something or that which constitutes a source of pride, boast" (BDAG 537, 1).

Paul himself writes about the judgment seat of Christ,[81] where the same thing takes place.

> "We will all stand before God's judgment seat.... So then, each of us will give an account of himself to God." (Romans 14:10, 12)

> "For we must all appear before the judgment seat of Christ, that each one may receive what is due him[82] for the things done while in the body, whether good or bad." (2 Corinthians 5:10)

To the Corinthians, Paul also writes about rewards – or none – on the Day of the Lord.

> "His work will be shown for what it is, because the Day will bring it to light. It will be revealed with fire, and the fire will test the quality of each man's work. If what he has built survives, he will receive his reward. If it is burned up, he will suffer loss; he himself will be saved, but only as one escaping through the flames." (1 Corinthians 3:13-15)

Note that our *reward* is determined at this time – not our *salvation*, which is based on grace, not works (Ephesians 2:8-9).

"Reward" in 1 Corinthians 3:14 is *misthos*, literally, "remuneration for work done, pay, wages," then by extension, "recognition (mostly by God) for the moral quality of an action, recompense." While the word can be used in an unfavorable sense as "requital" for the wicked, it usually positive, referring to our rewards in heaven.[83] For example, Jesus says, "great is your reward in heaven" (Matthew 5:12), a "reward from your Father in heaven" (Matthew 6:1), "a righteous man's reward" (Matthew 10:41), a reward for labor in church planting (1 Corinthians 3:8, 14), "rewarded fully" for a conscientious Christian life (2 John 8). The rewards are distributed at Christ's coming, "rewarding your servants the prophets" (Revelation 11:18), probably at the "judgment seat of Christ."

By now you may be feeling rather uncomfortable. That's because the idea of receiving rewards for our good works here on earth is embarrassing to modern-day Christians for two reasons:

1. Free grace. First, some of us have been so indoctrinated concerning God's free grace that rewards for "works" don't seem to fit into our theology. However, rewards (payments for work done) are nearly always distinguished in Scripture from salvation

---

[81] The judgment seat of Christ sounds suspiciously like the Great White Throne judgment of Revelation 20:12, where people are judged "according to their works." I know that Bible teachers say these are separate judgments, one for rewards and the other for salvation, but I think that's a bit arbitrary.

[82] *Komizō*, "to come into possession of something or experience something, carry off, get (for oneself), receive," frequently as recompense. In 2 Corinthians 5:10, "receive a recompense" (BDAG 557, 3).

[83] *Misthos*, BDAG 653, 2a.

(freely offered by God's grace). Paul clearly differentiates them in Ephesians 2:8-9 and 1 Corinthians 3:13-15.

Salvation by grace is the rock solid foundation that we do not lose, because it is anchored by our faith in the finished redemption of Christ on the cross as a sacrifice for our sins. Rewards for works are the "icing on the cake."

To work for rewards seems somehow unappreciative of the freeness of God's grace in salvation. Salvation seems like enough – more than enough, all we could ever ask or think. But no matter how you or I might feel emotionally, the New Testament clearly teaches that there will be rewards *in addition to* the gift of salvation, when Christ returns.

2. Sincere love. Second, we pride ourselves on serving out of pure love for God, not for any gain. Surely, obeying the first commandment, to "love the Lord your God with all your heart and with all your soul and with all your mind" (Matthew 22:37) should be the motivation for our work – our "labors of love," as we call them.

But in spite of that love, Jesus – and his Apostles Paul and John – teach us that we will be rewarded for our labors.

Paul is concerned that his converts continue in their faith so that he won't have labored "for nothing" (Philippians 2:16; 1 Thessalonians 3:5). Yes, Paul loves God supremely, but he is looking forward to glorying in these "trophies of grace," when Christ appears, much like the master in the Parable of the Talents, who invites the faithful servant to "enter into the joy of your master," to join in the welcome-home party that is going on inside the house in celebration of the master's return (Matthew 25:21). Indeed, their faithful service is an indication that these servants loved their master, just as the refusal to use the "talent" given him is an indication of the unfaithful servant's hatred for his master (Matthew 25:24-26).

Q1. (1 Thessalonians 2:19-20) How can we justify a desire for rewards for our labor in light of God's free gift of salvation and our love for him? What does Christ reward? What doesn't he reward? Why should showing accountability to our Master bring us pleasure? How does it motivate us?
http://www.joyfulheart.com/forums/index.php?showtopic=1223

The free salvation should just be the start of our Christian journey.
Christ rewards those who work & witness for him.
doesnt reward work we do for recognition here on earth.
It draws us closer to him.
It gives us a desire to work for him

When Jesus Comes (2:19)

The phrase, "at his coming" (NRSV, KJV) or "when he comes" (NIV) in 2:19 represents the earliest use of the noun *parousia* in the New Testament to refer to the Second Coming of Christ. "Coming" is *parousia*, "coming, advent." This word became the official term for a visit of a person of high rank, especially of kings and emperors visiting a province.[84] We also see this term in 1 Thessalonians 3:13; 4:15; and 2 Thessalonians 2:1, 8, 9. The Coming of Christ is a major theme of both Thessalonian letters. We'll consider this theme further in Lesson 5 on 1 Thessalonians 4:13-5:11.

Sent Timothy from Athens to Strengthen the Thessalonians (3:1-5)

Now we move from a teaching portion of the letter to a narrative one. The warm heart of a disciple-maker is clear in this passage.

> "[1] So when we[85] could stand it[86] no longer, we thought it best to be left by ourselves in Athens. [2] We sent Timothy, who is our brother and God's fellow worker in spreading the gospel of Christ, to strengthen and encourage you in your faith, [3] so that no one would be unsettled[87] by these trials.[88] You know quite well that we were destined for them. [4] In fact, when we were with you, we kept telling you that we would be persecuted. And it turned out that way, as you well know." (1 Thessalonians 3:1-4)

The suspense is killing Paul. Have the Thessalonian believers survived persecution with their faith intact? Paul dispatches Timothy from Athens to find out. Timothy doesn't catch up with Paul until he gets to Corinth (18:5). Timothy is just a young man, but he is given this important assignment. Paul can't return to Thessalonica because he had been declared *persona non grata* by the city leaders, but Timothy has a lower profile and can "fly under the radar" without raising trouble for the church.

Timothy is described here in two ways:

---

[84] *Parousia*, BDAG 780, 2bα.

[85] The "we" in 3:1 is apparently the "epistolary we." In 3:1 Paul uses "we," but in 3:5 he uses "I." There are a number of other examples of such a shift between "we" and "I" in Paul's writings. (See, for example, Romans 1:1 with 1:5; 2 Corinthians 1:15-2:13 with 2:14-4:18). We also see this in 3 John 9-10 and in secular writings of the period (Stott, *Message*, pp. 71-74).

[86] "Stand it" (NIV), "bear it" (NRSV), "forbear" (KJV) is *stegō*, "to bear up against difficulties, bear, stand, endure" (BDAG 942, 2).

[87] "Unsettled" (NIV), "shaken" (NRSV), "moved" (KJV) is *sainō*, "to shake," here figuratively, "to cause to be emotionally upset, move, disturb, agitate." Danker says that some take this to refer to the primary meaning of dogs, "wag the tail," hence "to try to win favor by an ingratiating manner, fawn upon, flatter" (BDAG 910, meanings 2 and 1). I think the idea of "shake" is preferable to "fawn upon."

[88] "Trials" (NIV), "persecutions" (NRSV), "afflictions" (KJV) is *thlipsis*. Literally it means, "pressure, pressing." Here it is used metaphorically as "trouble that inflicts distress, oppression, affliction, tribulation" (BDAG 457, 1).

1. "Brother," and
2. "God's fellow worker" (NIV) or "co-worker for God" (NRSV). The word here is *synergos*, "pertaining to working together with, helping," a "helper, fellow-worker."[89]

You may not have thought about it, but perhaps *you* could be described in the same way: a brother or sister who works in God's cause alongside great men and women of God. You are a valued co-worker or co-laborer of God's! The field of Timothy's labor is spreading or proclaiming[90] the gospel of Christ. I hope that is your focus too.

Notice Timothy's assignment in this return mission:

> "To strengthen and encourage you in your faith, so that no one would be unsettled by these trials." (3:2b-3a)

Persecution is difficult, especially for new believers. Paul is concerned that the pressure would be too much for this new church, so Timothy's role is to "strengthen and encourage."

- **"Strengthen"** (NIV, NRSV), "establish" (KJV) is *stērizō*. The basic meaning is "to fix firmly in a place, set up, establish, support." Here it is used figuratively, "to cause to be inwardly firm or committed, confirm, establish, strengthen."[91]
- **"Encourage"** (NIV, NRSV), "comfort" (KJV) is *parakaleō*, a word that has a wide scope: "to urge strongly, appeal to, urge, exhort, encourage" as well as "to instill someone with courage or cheer, comfort, encourage, cheer up."[92]

Timothy is to be a strengthener and encourager on behalf of Paul.

Q2. (2 Thessalonians 3:2-3) Why is Timothy's role to be a strengthener and encourager so important? In what ways was this a sensitive role. How did it help Timothy to be sent on this assignment? How does delegating ministry help the overall enterprise of the Kingdom? *It was a new church & they faced persecution*

http://www.joyfulheart.com/forums/index.php?showtopic=1224

Send two
Timothy grew with this assignment.
must delegate — one person can't do everything

---

[89] There is some confusion in what is the original Greek wording. A few ancient manuscripts read "co-worker of/for God" (D* 33 it[d, 85*]), which seems to be the reading that best explains the others. Most ancient texts read "servant (*diakonos*) of God (Aleph A P Ψ vg cop etc.). Later, some texts (D[c] K *Byz Lect* syr) conflated both readings as did the Textus Receptus which lies behind the KJV (Metzger, *Textual Commentary*, p. 631).

[90] "Spreading" (NIV), "proclaiming" (NRSV) does not appear in the Greek text but is implied.

[91] *Stērizō*, BDAG 945, 2. We see this word also in 3:13, and 2 Thessalonians 2:17 and 3:3.

[92] *Parakaleō*, BDAG 765, 2 and 4.

Destined for Persecution (3:3-4)

So Timothy is sent,

> "3 ... so that no one would be unsettled by these trials. You know quite well that we were destined for them. 4 In fact, when we were with you, we kept telling you that we would be persecuted.[93] And it turned out that way, as you well know." (3:3-4)

Paul talks about the "trials" (NIV), "persecutions" (NRSV), "afflictions" (KJV). The word is *thlipsis,* that we saw in 1:6 and will see again in 2 Thessalonians 1:6 – literally, "pressing, pressure." Here it is used in a metaphorical sense, "trouble that inflicts distress, oppression, affliction, tribulation."[94]

Sometimes when we suffer persecution and trouble we ask, "What did I do to deserve that?" That's the wrong question. A better one might be, "What did Jesus do to deserve being crucified?"

Jesus said,

> "10 Blessed are those who are persecuted because of righteousness,
> for theirs is the kingdom of heaven.
> 11 Blessed are you when people insult you,
> persecute you
> and falsely say all kinds of evil against you because of me.
> 12 Rejoice and be glad, because great is your reward in heaven,
> for in the same way they persecuted the prophets who were before you."
> (Matthew 5:10-12)

In other words, we should have joy because our persecution means that people see enough of Christ in us to be worth persecuting. We have good company in our persecutions – Christ and the honored Old Testament prophets. Elsewhere, Paul himself expresses blessing in suffering with Christ. He prays,

> "I want to know Christ and the power of his resurrection and **the fellowship of sharing in his sufferings**, becoming like him in his death...." (Philippians 3:10)

For the Christian, persecution isn't some kind of anomaly. We are *destined*[95] for persecutions (3:3b). As Paul later encourages Timothy, who is himself feeling a bit timid in the face of persecution,

---

[93] "Be persecuted" (NIV), "suffer persecution/tribulation" (NRSV, KJV) is *thlibō,* from the same root as "persecution" (*thlipsis*) in verse 3. The verb means "to cause to be troubled, oppress, afflict" (BDAG 457, 3).

[94] *Thlipsis,* BDAG 457, 1.

[95] "Destined for" (NIV, NRSV), "appointed thereunto" (KJV) is *keimai,* "lie, recline," here by extension, "be appointed, set, destined for something" (BDAG 537, 3a).

50 | 1 and 2 Thessalonians: Discipleship Lessons

"In fact, everyone who wants to live a godly life in Christ Jesus will be persecuted."[96] (2 Timothy 3:12)

Persecution is the lot of all Christians – some more, some less. Get used to it!

The Tempter Who Is Behind Persecution (3:5)

Paul knows that Satan, the tempter, has been hard at work. He tempted Jesus in the wilderness and was behind Jesus' persecution and betrayal (Luke 23:3; John 13:27). Paul knows that this is a spiritual battle, that we humans are vulnerable.

"For this reason, when I could stand it no longer, I sent to find out about your faith. I was afraid[97] that in some way the tempter[98] might have tempted you and our efforts[99] might have been useless.[100]" (3:5)

God tries us to examine and refine our character. But Satan tries us to try to get us to fall. Here Satan is referred to as the "chief tempter," as he is elsewhere as well (Matthew 4:1-3; 1 Corinthians 7:5; Revelation 2:10).

Q3. (1 Thessalonians 3:3-5) In what ways does persecution discourage Christians from active, open service? In what ways does it mature them? In what ways does it reveal our underlying motives? Why do you think God allows the tempter the ability to tempt us? Why hasn't he done away with Satan already?

http://www.joyfulheart.com/forums/index.php?showtopic=1225

We are turned - afraid
It matures us as a christian because Christ said
it would happen + in the end we will be blessed.
I don't know!
All in his time

Timothy Returns with Good News (3:6)

What a relief it must have been for Paul when Timothy returned with a good report!

---

[96] *Diōkō*, "to harass someone, especially because of beliefs, persecute" (BDAG 254, 2).

[97] "I was afraid that" (NIV, NRSV), "lest" (KJV) is *mēpōs*, "marker of a negative perspective expressing misgiving," frequently rendered "lest" (BDAG 902, 2b).

[98] "Tempter" and "tempt" both translate the verb *peirazō*, "try," here negatively, "to entice to improper behavior, tempt" (BDAG 793, 4).

[99] "Efforts" (NIV), "labor" (NRSV, KJV) is *kopos*, "work, labor, toil" (BDAG 558, 2).

[100] "Useless" (NIV), "in vain" (NRSV, KJV) is *kenos*, "empty," here, "pertaining to being without purpose or result, in vain" (BDAG 539, 3).

> "But Timothy has just now come to us from you and has brought good news about your faith and love. He has told us that you always have pleasant memories of us and that you long[101] to see us, just as we also long to see you." (3:6)

Timothy reports on their:

1. Faith
2. Love
3. Pleasant memories
4. Longing to see Paul

When you're away from someone you love and receive no word from them, your mind can go crazy exploring scenarios of the worst that could happen. But now Paul is reassured, both about the Thessalonians' Christian faith and their intense love for him.

Paul's Delight in the Thessalonians' Faith (3:7-10)

In the next verses you get a hint of Paul's personal involvement in these children in the gospel:

> "7 Therefore, brothers, in all our distress[102] and persecution[103] we were encouraged[104] about you because of your faith. 8 For now we really live, since you are standing firm in the Lord. 9 How can we thank God enough for you in return for all the joy we have in the presence of our God because of you? 10 Night and day we pray most earnestly that we may see you again and supply what is lacking in your faith." (3:8-10)

Paul is undergoing struggles in Corinth, but word from these dear believers heartens him. The recent news has him thanking God and praying constantly that he can return to Thessalonica.

Paul's expression in 3:8 is a bit confusing:

> "For now we really live, since you are standing firm[105] in the Lord." (3:8)

---

[101] "Long" (NIV, NRSV), "desiring greatly" (KJV) is *epipotheō*, "to have a strong desire for something, with implication of need, long for, desire," from *epi-* "motion, approach, direction toward or to anything" + *potheō*, "to yearn" (Thayer, 243 and 233, D2).

[102] "Distress" (NIV, NRSV), "affliction" (KJV) is *thlipsis* that we saw in verse 3.

[103] "Persecution" (NIV, NRSV), "distress" (KJV) is *anankē*, "a state of distress or trouble, distress, calamity, pressure" (BDAG 61, 2).

[104] "Encouraged" (NIV, NRSV), "comforted" (KJV) is *parakaleō* (which we saw in 3:2), "to instill someone with courage or cheer, comfort, encourage, cheer up" (BDAG 765, 4).

[105] "Stand firm / stand fast" is *stēkō*, "to be firmly committed in conviction or belief, stand firm, be steadfast" (BDAG 944, 2).

He's not talking about spiritual life. It's just an expression describing his high level of encouragement. We might say, "a breath of fresh air" or "*now* we're living!" Wanamaker notes that Paul "derives a sense of strength from the endurance of his converts that enables him to continue his missionary work in the face of opposition and oppression"[106]

In 3:10 you can sense the intensity of his prayer to return to see his dear friends there.

> "Night and day we pray most earnestly[107] that we may see you again and supply what is lacking[108] in your faith. [11] Now may our God and Father himself and our Lord Jesus clear the way[109] for us to come to you." (3:10-11)

When he says he wants to "supply what is lacking in your faith," he doesn't mean it as a criticism. "Supply" (NIV), "restore" (NRSV), "perfect" (KJV) is *katartizō*, "to cause to be in a condition to function well, put in order, restore," with the idea of "put into proper condition."[110] Paul's passion is to bring each believer to his potential. To the church at Colossae he wrote:

> "We proclaim him, admonishing and teaching everyone with all wisdom, so that we may present everyone perfect in Christ." (Colossians 1:28)

To the Romans, whom he has not yet visited, he wrote later on:

> "I long to see you so that I may impart to you some spiritual gift to make you strong...." (Romans 1:11)

We shouldn't see this as pride so much as Paul's confidence that God will work through him to strengthen people in the faith wherever he goes. Oh, how he wants to return to Thessalonica! Unfortunately, he doesn't get to do so for another five years.

Q4. (1 Thessalonians 3:10-11; Romans 1:11) What is the value of visits of special speakers to a congregation? What can they impart that your regular pastor can't? Why

---

[106] Wanamaker, *1&2 Thessalonians*, p. 136.

[107] "Pray most earnestly" (NIV, NRSV), "praying exceedingly" (KJV) is two words, *deomai*, "to ask for something pleadingly, ask, request," (BDAG 18, b), and *hyperekperissou*, "quite beyond all measure," a compounding of three words to create the highest form of comparison imaginable. This superlative also appears at Ephesians 3:20 – "immeasurably more than all we ask or imagine.." (BDAG 1033).

[108] "Lacking" is *hysterēma*, "a defect that must be removed so that perfection can be attained, lack, shortcoming" (BDAG 1044, 2).

[109] "Clear the way" (NIV), "direct our way" (NRSV, KJV) is two words: *hodos*, "way" and *kateuthynō*, literally "make/keep straight." Here, figuratively, "lead, direct" (BDAG 532). These words render a Hebrew expression familiar from the Old Testament, especially in this verse: "In all thy ways acknowledge him, and he shall direct (literally, 'make straight') thy paths" (Proverbs 3:6, KJV).

[110] *Katartizō*, BDAG 526, 1b.

is a ministry of itinerant preaching so difficult – and important?
http://www.joyfulheart.com/forums/index.php?showtopic=1226

they make friends & converts + then go on to another place + do it over again.

A Brief Prayer (3:11-13)

As Paul closes this section of the letter, he offers a brief benediction, asking God to do for them remotely what Paul longed to do for them in person through his ministry.

> "[12] May the Lord make your love increase and overflow[111] for each other and for everyone else, just as ours does for you. [13] May he strengthen[112] your hearts so that you will be blameless[113] and holy[114] in the presence of our God and Father when our Lord Jesus comes with all his holy ones." (3:11-13)

Notice Paul's strong expectation of the coming[115] of Christ Jesus. It will be an awesome day of judgment as we're are ushered in God's presence – that's why Paul prays for blameless and holy hearts on that Day!

Christ's coming will also be a day of glory when King Jesus comes with "all his holy ones" (NIV) or "all his saints" (NRSV, KJV). As we'll see in Lesson 5 on 4:14, Christ isn't returning alone. His coming will be sudden, but not silent. He will come "with a loud command, with the voice of the archangel and with the trumpet call of God (4:16). Hallelujah!

Lessons for Disciples

In these verses we've formed a picture of Paul's heart.

- Great love and longing for his spiritual children.
- Expectation of rewards for his disciple-making ministry at Christ's coming.
- Willingness to delegate ministry duties to his assistant Timothy.

---

[111] "Overflow" (NIV), "abound" (NRSV, KJV) is *perisseuō*, "to cause something to exist in abundance, cause to abound" (BDAG 805, 2b).

[112] "Strengthen" (NIV, NRSV), "stablish" (KJV) is *stērizō* (that we saw in 3:2), "to cause to be inwardly firm or committed, confirm, establish, strengthen" (BDAG 945, 2).

[113] "Blameless" (NIV, NRSV), "unblameable" (KJV) is *amemptos* (of which we saw in adverb in 2:10), "blameless, faultless," from *a-*, "not" + *memphomai*, "to blame" (BDAG 52).

[114] "Holy" (NIV), "holiness" (NRSV, KJV) is *hagiōsynē*, "holiness" (BDAG 11), "moral purity" (Thayer, 42, 2).

[115] "Comes/coming" is *parousia*, "coming, advent." This word became the official term for a visit of a person of high rank, especially of kings and emperors visiting a province" (BDAG 780, 2bα).

- Endurance of persecution as our lot as believers in this world.

- Delight in the growth and increasing maturity of his spiritual children.

May God work in us some of these qualities as we seek to make a difference in our world!

Prayer

Father, thank you for what we've seen of Paul's heart for disciple-making. We ask you to impart to us the same kind of passion and love for the ministry you've called us to. In Jesus' name, we pray. Amen.

Key Verses

"For what is our hope, our joy, or the crown in which we will glory in the presence of our Lord Jesus when he comes? Is it not you? Indeed, you are our glory and joy." (1 Thessalonians 2:19-20)

"May he strengthen your hearts so that you will be blameless and holy in the presence of our God and Father when our Lord Jesus comes with all his holy ones." (1 Thessalonians 3:13)

4. The Command and Blessing of Holy Sex (1 Thessalonians 4:1-12)

Up to now, Paul has been praising the Thessalonian church and sharing how very much he loves them. But here we have a transition. Paul comes to the meat of the letter.

Aiming at a God-Pleasing Life (4:1-2)

"[1] Finally, brothers, we instructed you how to live in order to please God, as in fact you are living. Now we ask you and urge you in the Lord Jesus to do this more and more. [2] For you know what instructions[116] we gave you by the authority of the Lord Jesus." (4:1-2)

1 Thessalonians contains three items in the category of "how to live"[117] – basic Christian ethics and lifestyle. In this lesson we'll see Paul's teachings on:

1. Sexual behavior (4:3-8)

2. Brotherly love (4:9-10)

3. Work rather than dependence (4:11-12)

Notice the goal of these instructions: to please God.[118] What a radical idea! Our world lives to please others and to please oneself, or to be a "good person" or a "good citizen." Non-believers set their own standards – or more commonly adapt to the standards of the culture around them. They keep up with the "speed of traffic," even if it is over the speed limit. But the Christian – one who loves Christ – patterns his or her life around what kind of behavior delights God.

You sometimes hear a negative slant on this – "my Catholic guilt." But that's wrong. Christianity is love-based, not guilt-based. For religious people who don't know God, all

---

[116] "Instructions" (NIV, NRSV), "commandments" (KJV) is *parangelia*, "an announcement respecting something that must be done, order, command, precept, advice, exhortation" (BDAG 760). The word translated "authority" (NIV) is not in the Greek text, but implied. "*Parangelia* was often used for either a military command or for a civil order, for example, by a court or by magistrates" (Stott, p. 78).

[117] "Live" (NIV, NRSV), "walk" (KJV) is *peripateō*, "to conduct one's life, comport oneself, behave, live as habit of conduct" (BDAG 803, 2a).

[118] "Please" is *areskō*, "to give pleasure/satisfaction, please, accommodate" (BDAG 129, 2a).

they're left with are rules. But to those of us who know and love God, our desire is to please him in all that we do.

Notice that Paul isn't just sharing ethics. He speaks with the authority of Jesus Christ Himself.

Q1. (1 Thessalonians 4:1-2) What is the difference between (1) conducting our lives by rules and (2) conducting our lives trying to please our God? Which is stronger? Rule-keeping or love? On whose authority does Paul bring these commands?
http://www.joyfulheart.com/forums/index.php?showtopic=1227

Most People keep the rules — Christians like to please God. Living to please God is much stronger from Jesus — authority of Lord Jesus

Sexual Immorality in the Greco-Roman World

The first of these lifestyle instructions or commandments relates to sexuality. Before we look at them, it's important to understand the context of Paul's world – especially the Greco-Roman world outside of Judea and Galilee. For these pagans, sex in marriage *only* was a very strange notion indeed. Various forms of extramarital union were tolerated. Some were even encouraged.

Demosthenes, considered to be the greatest orator of ancient Greece (384-322 BC), once said famously,

> "We have mistresses for pleasure, concubines to care for our daily body's needs, and wives to bear us legitimate children and to be faithful guardians of our households."[119]

These are the categories.

1. **Mistress.** As well as sex, she might provide intellectual companionship.
2. **Concubine.** Sex was common with one's household slaves, as they were considered the owner's property to do with whatever he wished.
3. **Harlot.** Prostitutes were available for casual sex. For example, archeologists have uncovered brothels in the ancient city of Pompey.
4. **Wife.** Rather than being a man's sole sexual partner, the wife's function was to manage his household and be the mother of his legitimate children and heirs.

Furthermore, there was no body of public opinion to discourage sexual immorality, though excesses might be made fun of in the same way you'd joke about a notorious

---

[119] Demosthenes, *Against Neaera* 122.

glutton or drunkard. A number of popular religions in the Mediterranean area involved ritual sex with temple prostitutes. In Thessalonica there was the cult of the Cabiri of Samothrace.[120] Ephesus was known for its Temple of Artemis. Corinth was famous for its temple of Aphrodite and notorious for its loose sexual morals.

Paul's converts at Thessalonica have probably been Christians for less than a year. Timothy has reported to Paul that sexual immorality is still going on, so Paul hits it hard in this letter. Bruce notes, "When the gospel was introduced into pagan society, it was necessary to emphasize the complete breach with accepted mores in this area, demanded by the new life in Christ."[121] As Paul writes to the Corinthians church a few years later, Christians must, "Shun fornication!" (1 Corinthians 6:18)

Holy and Honorable Sex (4:3-8)

In thoroughly immoral Thessalonica, the Christian lifestyle stands out. Paul writes to the Thessalonians:

> "3 It is God's will that you should be sanctified: that you should avoid sexual immorality; 4 that each of you should learn to control his own body in a way that is holy and honorable, 5 not in passionate lust like the heathen, who do not know God; 6 and that in this matter no one should wrong his brother or take advantage of him. The Lord will punish men for all such sins, as we have already told you and warned you. 7 For God did not call us to be impure, but to live a holy life. 8 Therefore, he who rejects this instruction does not reject man but God, who gives you his Holy Spirit." (4:3-8)

Notice four things about this passage:

1.   God is in favor of sex – after all, he invented it;

2.   God's will and a relationship with God are very much involved with our sexuality (verse 3a, 4b, 7a-8);

3.   Sanctification and holiness are a high priority (verse 3a, 4b, 7b); and

4.   God judges sexual immorality severely as rebellion against Him (verse 6b).

Many Greeks held a strict dualism between body and spirit. What was done in the body had no relationship to one's spirit, thus immoral sex didn't affect one's spiritual life. Not so in Christian teaching! Let's examine this passage in detail.

---

[120] This section draws heavily on the insights of FF Bruce, *1&2 Thessalonians*, p. 82.
[121] Bruce, *1&2 Thessalonians*, p. 82.

Sexual Immorality (4:3)

> "It is God's will that you should be sanctified: that you should avoid sexual immorality." (4:3)

Paul commands the believers to "avoid" (NIV), "abstain from" (NRSV, KJV) sexual immorality.[122] This phrase is similar to Acts 15:20, 29, in the letter from the Jerusalem Council that Silas had been charged to carry to the Gentile churches.

"Sexual immorality" (NIV), "fornication" (NRSV, KJV) is *porneia*, "unlawful sexual intercourse, prostitution, unchastity, fornication."[123] Bruce observes, "While *porneia* means primarily traffic in harlots (*pornai*), it may denote any form of illicit sexual relationship."[124] Homosexuality would also be included in this term. While we're defining terms, "chastity" in English is, "abstention from unlawful sexual intercourse." However, it's basic sense does *not* mean refraining from sexual intercourse within marriage. "Fornication," (the KJV translation of *porneia*) means in English, "consensual sexual intercourse between two persons not married to each other."[125] It usually refers to unmarried persons. Adultery, on the other hand, refers to extramarital affairs of individuals who are married.

I once had a couple in my church who were itching to get married. The man, a sincere new Christian, told me that he didn't see anything in the Bible that said having sex with your fiancée before marriage was sinful. He didn't read carefully – maybe because he didn't want to. That command is here in 1 Thessalonians 4 and elsewhere in the New Testament, such as in 1 Corinthians 7.

Sanctification and Holiness

Paul isn't condemning sex. But he commands that sexual intercourse be practiced strictly in marriage, as is God's revealed will.

> "³ It is God's will that you should be sanctified (*hagiasmos*): that you should avoid sexual immorality; ⁴ that each of you should learn to control his own body in a way that is holy (*hagiasmos*) and honorable...." (4:3-4)

---

[122] The verb is *apechomai*, "to avoid contact with or use of something, keep away, abstain, refrain from" (BDAG 103, 5).

[123] *Porneia*, BDAG 854, 1. "*Porneia* ... and its cognates as used by Paul denote any kind of illegitimate – extramarital and unnatural – sexual intercourse or relationship" (David F. Wright, "Sexuality, Sexual Ethics," *DPL*, pp. 871-875).

[124] Bruce, *1&2 Thessalonians*, p. 82.

[125] *Merriam-Webster's 11th Collegiate Dictionary.*

The noun translated "sanctified/sanctification" is *hagiasmos*, "personal dedication to the interests of the deity, holiness, consecration, sanctification."[126] It is used in the New Testament in a moral sense for a process or, more often (as in 4:3), its result, that is, the state of being made holy. This process is also known as "sanctification."

The concept of holiness begins in the Old Testament. From earliest times, God had commanded, "Be holy, because I am holy" (Leviticus 11:45b). Holiness is not an option.

> "You are to be holy (*qādôsh*) to me because I, the LORD, am holy, and I have set you apart from the nations to be my own." (Leviticus 20:26)

The basic meaning of the Hebrew root *qadosh* seems to be "to divide, to cut, to separate." So the underlying concept of holiness is to separate for His exclusive use God's own people and possessions from the common and secular.[127] In the Old Testament, for example, the priests were dedicated to the Lord. So were priests' garments, the tabernacle, and the sacrifices to be offered, such as the showbread and animal sacrifices. The high priest wore a gold plate on his turban bearing the words "Holy to the Lord" (Exodus 39:30). Sometimes spoils of war were also dedicated to the Lord.

God's people in both the Old and New Testaments are called "saints" or "holy ones" (Hebrew *qādôsh* or *ḥāsîd*; Greek *hagios*).

In the New Testament, the idea of holiness or sanctification has two aspects:

1. We *are* holy positionally.[128] We are holy because we are "in Christ," because we are part of Christ.

> "For he chose us **in him** before the creation of the world to be **holy and blameless** in his sight. In love he predestined us to be adopted as his sons through Jesus Christ, in accordance with his pleasure and will – to the praise of his glorious grace, which he has freely given us **in the One** he loves." (Ephesians 1:4-6)

In this sense, sanctification and justification are closely aligned in a number of New Testament verses that refer to Christ's finished work on the cross.[129]

2. We are *becoming* holy experientially.[130] We are being changed day-by-day into Christ's likeness as we focus on Christ (2 Corinthians 3:18). We are to strive for holiness

---

[126] *Hagiasmos*, BDAG 10.

[127] Otto Procksch, *hagios, ktl.*, TDNT 1:88-97, 100-115, especially, p. 89. *Qādash*, TWOT #1990a.

[128] White calls this aspect of sanctification, "status conferred" (R.E.O. White, "Sanctification," in Walter A. Elwell (editor), *Evangelical Dictionary of Theology* (Baker, 1984), pp. 969-971.

[129] 1 Corinthians 1:2, 30; 6:11; Ephesians 5:25-26; 2 Thessalonians 2:13; 1 Peter 1:1-2; Hebrews 2:11; 9:13-14; 10:10, 14, 29; 13:12.

[130] White calls this aspect of sanctification, "process pursued." Rudolph Bultmann proposed that the imperative (ethical command) proceeds out of the indicative (statement of theological truth), with the idea

(Hebrews 12:14). This is an ongoing process of perfection that works out in our experience as we yield to the Holy Spirit. The fruit of the Spirit (Galatians 5:22-23) is the product of this sanctification process. This second sense of holiness and sanctification is clear in a number of other New Testament passages.[131] In 1 Thessalonians, we see this second sense especially. Here are two other passages in this letter that use the concept.

> "May he strengthen your hearts so that you will be blameless and **holy** (*hagiōsynē*) in the presence of our God and Father when our Lord Jesus comes with all his **holy ones** (*hagios*)." (3:13)

> "It is God's will that you should be **sanctified** (*hagiasmos*): that you should avoid sexual immorality; that each of you should learn to control his own body in a way that is **holy** (*hagiasmos*) and honorable...." (4:3-4)

> "May God himself, the God of peace, **sanctify** (*hagiazō*) you through and through. May your whole spirit, soul and body be kept blameless at the coming of our Lord Jesus Christ. The one who calls you is faithful and he will do it." (5:23-24)

Q2. (1 Thessalonians 4:3-4) What does it mean to be "sanctified"? In what sense are we "holy" now? In what sense are we in the process of becoming "holy"? What does holiness have to do with our sexuality?

http://www.joyfulheart.com/forums/index.php?showtopic=1228

Controlling Ourselves Sexually (4:4-5)

God desires us to live holy lives. This is not tangential to sexuality, but very much involves our personal sexuality. Paul commands:

> "[3] It is God's will ... that you should avoid sexual immorality; [4] that each of you should learn to control his own body in a way that is holy and honorable, [5] not in passionate lust like the heathen, who do not know God." (4:3-5)

Verse 4 is especially hard to render accurately in English, because the key Greek word can be interpreted two ways. Here are two representative translations:

---

that Christians should "become what they are" (cited in Stanley E. Porter, "Holiness, Sanctification," DPL, p. 401).

[131] Philippians 3:12; Romans 6:19, 22; 8:29-30; 12:1-2; 2 Corinthians 7:1; 1 Timothy 2:15; 1 John 3:1-3, etc.

"Every one of you should know how to **possess his vessel** in sanctification and honor." (KJV, NASB)

"Each of you should learn to **control his own body** in a way that is holy and honorable." (NIV, NRSV)

Let's consider the arguments for each translation.

1. Possess his vessel, that is, his wife. The verb *ktaomai* means "to gain possession of, procure for oneself, acquire, get."[132] Indeed, the Greek Septuagint translation of the Old Testament (about 200 BC) uses this word for acquiring a wife in Ruth 4:10 and in the Apocryphal book of Sirach 36:29.

The noun translated "vessel" (KJV), "body" (NIV, NRSV) is *skeuos*, first, "thing, object," then, "a container of any kind, jar," and here, "a human being exercising a function, instrument, vessel."[133] To interpret this phrase as acquiring or possessing one's own wife follows Rabbinical usage, and was adopted by Church Fathers Theodore of Mopsuestia and Augustine.[134] However, in 1 Peter 3:7, *both* husband and wife are considered vessels, the wife being the "weaker" one.

2. Control one's body, specifically, one's sexual organs. The other option is to interpret *skeuos* in its common sense as "vessel, tool, implement, instrument."[135] That seems to be the Hebraic use in 1 Samuel 21:5, where the high priest asks David, "Have the men kept themselves from women?" and he answers, "The young men's vessels are holy." Church Fathers Tertullian and Chrysostom both interpreted *skeuos*, "vessel," as referring to one's own body. In fact, *skeuos*, was recognized euphemism in ancient Greek for the genital organs of both males and females.[136] Wanamaker argues that the Thessalonians wouldn't have understood a Rabbinical reference to "vessel" as wife; if Paul intended to mean "wife" for these readers, he would have used *gunē*, "woman,

---

[132] *Ktaomai*, BDAG 572, 1.

[133] *Skeuos*, BDAG 927, 3.

[134] In Maurer's study of *skeuos*, he concludes that "the underlying phrases, 'to use as a vessel,' 'to make one's vessel,' etc. are to be regarded as established euphemisms for sexual intercourse." For 1 Thessalonians 4:4 Maurer sees it likely that any bilingual Jew would interpret this as "hold his wife" (that is, "live with his wife") in holiness and honor. Paul doesn't show any acquaintance with the idea of the body as the container of the soul or the individual ego (Christian Maurer, *skeuos*, TDNT 7:361-362, 365-367, especially p. 362).

[135] Wanamaker, *1&2 Thessalonians*, pp. 152-153. Wanamaker argues that "wife" wouldn't likely be the meaning of *skeuos*, since the context is sexual immorality.

[136] Henry George Liddell and Robert Scott, *A Greek-English Lexicon* (revised and augmented throughout by. Sir Henry Stuart Jones. with the assistance of. Roderick McKenzie; Oxford: Clarendon Press, 1940), p. 1607, which cites *Antistius Grammaticus* 4.243 and Aelian, *De Natura Animalium*.17.11. It means the same as = *aidoion* ("privy parts, pudenda, both of men and women").

wife." Without a Jewish background, they would have taken *skeuos* as referring to sexual organs. In this case, the verb *ktaomai*, has the nuance, "to gain control or mastery," and could apply equally to men or women.

Taking "vessel" as a euphemism for sexual organs makes the most sense to me. But, however, you take it, Paul is pretty clear: we are commanded to keep our sexual urges under control, so that our sexual lives are conducted with "holiness (*hagiasmos*) and honor[137]" (4:4b, NRSV). This is the second of three references to holiness in this passage.

Paul contrasts "holiness and honor" with "not in passionate lust like the heathen, who do not know God." "Passionate lust" (NIV), "lustful passion" (NRSV) or "the lust of concupiscence[138]" (KJV) consists of two words in Greek: *pathos*, "experience of strong desire, passion,"[139] and *epithymia*, "a desire for something forbidden or simply inordinate, craving, lust," here, of sexual desire.[140] Certainly, sexual intercourse involves physical passion – God made us this way. But that passion needs to be under control and channeled exclusively towards our spouse. A river flow can be powerful, especially when it is contained by banks on both sides to protect from flood. As Solomon wrote with erotic imagery a thousand years before Paul:

> "May your fountain[141] be blessed,
> and may you rejoice in the wife of your youth.
> A loving doe, a graceful deer –
> may her breasts satisfy[142] you always,
> may you ever be captivated by her love.
> Why be captivated, my son, by an adulteress?
> Why embrace the bosom of another man's wife?
> For a man's ways are in full view of the LORD,
> and he examines all his paths." (Proverbs 5:18-21)

---

[137] "Honor" is *timē*, "manifestation of esteem, honor, reverence." If our passage refers to a female member of the household, then this connotation is "the showing of honor, reverence, or respect." If it refers to one's body, then the connotation is as a state of being, "respectability" (BDAG 1005, 2a or c).

[138] The English word "concupiscence" means "strong desire, especially sexual desire." (*Merriam-Webster's 11th Collegiate Dictionary*).

[139] *Pathos*, BDAG 748, 2.

[140] *Epithymia*, BDAG 372, 2.

[141] "Fountain" is *māqôr*, a euphemism for the womb, both as "a fountain of blood, but also as the fountain from which children issue" (Leonard J. Coppes, *māqôr*, TWOT #2004a).

[142] "Satisfy" is *rāwâ*, "be satiated, have one's fill," also used of adulterous sexual intercourse (Proverbs 7:18).

The "passionate lust like the heathen,[143] who do not know God," is selfish – satisfying one's own sexual needs only. It isn't faithful. It doesn't care about the consequences. It involves only animalistic satisfaction, not the sexual bonding of committed love between a husband and wife.

Q3. (1 Thessalonians 4:3-5) Are humans actually capable of controlling their sexual urges? If so, why are so many people seemingly out of control? Why is it important to control ourselves sexually within marriage? What happens when sexuality does not have any boundaries? What happens to marriages, to children, to our spirits, to our bodies?

http://www.joyfulheart.com/forums/index.php?showtopic=1229

yes – the easy way out – one woman – Devorse – desease – marage lost – Children unhapy – Sinks Low.

Wronging or Taking Advantage of a Brother (4:6a)

"... and that in this matter[144] no one should wrong his brother or take advantage of him." (4:6a)

Paul is probably referring to sexual cheating or adultery within the Christian community here, since he uses the term "brother."[145] To sleep with another man's wife or fiancé would be to "wrong him" or trespass against him.[146] It also involves cheating, doing something behind one's back.[147] If a man were to have sex with an unmarried woman in the Christian community, in a sense he would be cheating her future husband.

---

[143] "Heathen" (NIV), "Gentiles" (NRSV, KJV) is *ethnos* (from which we get our word "ethnic"), "nation, people," here in the sense of "foreigners, unbelievers" (BDAG 277, 2b).

[144] "Matter" is *pragma,* "matter or concern of any kind, thing, matter, affair," here, probably as a euphemism for an "(illicit sexual) affair" (BDAG 859, 3).

[145] "Brother" (NIV, KJV), "brother or sister" (NRSV) is *adelphos,* "brother." In the plural it can refer to both males and females. Here is refers to "a person viewed as a brother in terms of a close affinity, brother, fellow member, member, associate" (BDAG 19, 2a).

[146] "Wrong" (NIV, NRSV), "go beyond" (KJV) is *hyperbainō,* here used in a moral sense "to transgress by going beyond proper limits in behavior, trespass, sin" (BDAG 1032, 2).

[147] "Take advantage of" (NIV), "exploit" (NRSV), "defraud" (KJV) is *pleonekteō.* The basic meaning is "to have more, or a greater part or share" (Thayer 516). Here, it connotes "to take advantage of, exploit, outwit, defraud, cheat someone" (BDAG 824, 1a).

Severe Punishment for Sexual Immorality (4:6b-8)

I've heard people say that sexual sins are no worse than any other kind of sins. And in a sense, any transgression against God's law makes one a lawbreaker, whether for a minor or major offence (James 2:10-11). But this argument is used only by those who seek to minimize their sin – not by God-fearing believers who desire to please God.

In this passage Paul, Christ's apostle, pronounces terrible punishments for sexual sins in particular.

> "The Lord will punish men for all such sins, as we have already told you and warned you. 7 For God did not call us to be impure, but to live a holy life. 8 Therefore, he who rejects this instruction does not reject man but God, who gives you his Holy Spirit." (4:6b-8)

Paul told the Colossian church that because of sexual immorality and adultery, "the wrath of God is coming" (Colossians 3:6).

There can be a high degree of self-deception and self-rationalization that a person uses to excuses him- or herself so as to continue in sexual sins. To members of other churches struggling with the same temptations, Paul is adamant:

> "Let no one **deceive** you with empty words, for because of such things God's wrath comes on those who are disobedient." (Ephesians 5:6)

> "Do you not know that the wicked will not inherit the kingdom of God? Do not be **deceived**...." (1 Corinthians 6:9a)

> "I warn you, as I did before, that those who live like this will not inherit the kingdom of God." (Galatians 5:21b)

Sexual sin was a "big deal" for new Christians in the immoral cities of the first century, just as it is a "big deal" for Christians today.

We can read such verses, realize our sins, and be overcome with fear of damnation. That isn't God's desire at all. Praise God, there is forgiveness for sins. As Paul told the Corinthians, some of whom had been fornicators, adulterers, and homosexual offenders:

> "You were washed, you were sanctified, you were justified in the name of the Lord Jesus Christ and by the Spirit of our God." (1 Corinthians 6:11)

If we adopt a sinful, debauched lifestyle, we are only kidding ourselves about the reality of our Christian faith. Of course, we are not saved by "acting holy." Rather, we are saved by the sacrifice of Jesus for our sins. But if we *are* saved, we will desire to be holy, and our lives will gradually become more and more like Christ. In our passage, Paul warns us:

> "The Lord will punish men for all such sins, as we have already told you and warned
> you." (4:6b)

Paul states this commandment with all certainty. Then he declares that God will act as the avenger, the one who punishes breaches of this kind. [148] He reminds them that he has both said this to them before,[149] and when he did so he had told them in no uncertain terms – he solemnly warned[150] them – concerning a holy Christian lifestyle and the punishment for breaching it. They are fully responsible for knowing the serious penalty for sexual sins.

Notice Paul's return to the theme of holiness as he concludes this section – the third of three times he uses this theme in this passage:

> "For God did not call us to be impure,[151] but to live a holy life."[152] (4:7)

Sex is to be holy because we – and our bodies – belong to the Lord. He told the Corinthian church:

> "The body is not meant for sexual immorality, but for the Lord, and the Lord for the
> body." (1 Corinthians 6:13)

This requires careful vigilance and self-discipline, especially for people new-from-the-world who are accustomed to practicing sexual immorality. Oswald Chambers observes.

> "If we do not sacrifice the natural to the spiritual, the natural life will resist and defy the
> life of the Son of God in us and will produce continual turmoil. This is always the result
> of an undisciplined spiritual nature. We go wrong because we stubbornly refuse to
> discipline ourselves physically, morally, or mentally. We excuse ourselves by saying,
> 'Well, I wasn't taught to be disciplined when I was a child.' Then discipline yourself
> now! If you don't, you will ruin your entire personal life for God."[153]

Paul concludes this passage with an extremely strong exhortation.

---

[148] "Will punish" (NIV), "is an avenger" (NRSV, KJV) is *ekdikos*, "pertaining to justice being done so as to rectify wrong done to another, punishing." Here it is used as a substantive, "one who punishes" (BDAG 303).

[149] *Proepō* or *prolegō*, "to say something in advance of an event, tell beforehand/ in advance" (BDAG 872, 1).

[150] "Warned" (NIV), "solemnly warned" (NRSV), "testified" (KJV) is *diamartyromai*, "to make a solemn declaration about the truth of something, testify of, bear witness to" (originally under oath), generally, to state something in such a way that the auditor is to be impressed with its seriousness. Perhaps even to the level of, "to exhort with authority in matters of extraordinary importance," frequently with reference to higher powers and/or suggestion of peril, solemnly urge, exhort, warn" (BDAG 233, 1 and 2).

[151] "Impure" (NIV), "impurity" (NRSV), "uncleanness" (KJV) is *akatharsia*, "unclean," here used figuratively, "a state of moral corruption, immorality, vileness," especially of sexual sins (BDAG 34, 2).

[152] "To live a holy life" (NIV), "in holiness" (NRSV, KJV) is *hagiasmos*, which we saw in 4:1.

[153] Oswald Chambers, *My Utmost for His Highest* (first published in 1927), reading for December 10th.

"He who rejects this instruction does not reject man but God, who gives you his Holy Spirit." (1 Thessalonians 4:8)

Paul is not talking about a slip-up in a one-time moment of weakness. He is talking about people who resist his teaching as if it were merely one man's opinion. Since Paul speaks for God, to disregard Paul's teaching constitutes rebellion[154] against God himself.

Is God against sex? Of course not! Is God against sexual fun in marriage. No. But unbridled sex outside of marriage is incompatible with holy living!

Q4. (1 Thessalonians 4:6-8) Why do you think Paul mentions such severe punishments for sexual immorality? Are these punishments more severe than for other sins? What effect should these warnings have on Christians?

http://www.joyfulheart.com/forums/index.php?showtopic=1230

God is strongly against sex other than with your spouse! no — but paul warns of Gods wrath. we should be strictly faithful to our spouse

Love for the Brothers (4:9-10)

Now Paul turns to his second point in writing the Thessalonians – love.

"9 About brotherly love we do not need to write to you, for you yourselves have been taught by God to love each other. 10 And in fact, you do love all the brothers throughout Macedonia. Yet we urge you, brothers, to do so more and more." (4:9-10)

Paul refers to two aspects of love in verse 9, both familial love and *"agapē love."* "Brotherly love" (NIV, KJV), "love for the brothers and sisters" (NRSV) is *philadelphia,* "love of a brother/sister," the love of those who are related by blood. In the New Testament it refers to love for brothers and sisters in the Christian community who are related by the blood of Christ.[155]

The second kind of love in this verse is *"agapē love."* The Greeks have several words for love.

1. *Erōs,* or erotic love, is often a selfish sort of love, concern for one who can do something for me.

---

[154] "Rejects" (NIV, NRSV), "despiseth" (KJV) is *atheteō,* "to reject something as invalid, declare invalid, nullify, ignore," and directed toward God, "to reject by not recognizing something or someone, reject, not recognize, disallow" (BDAG 24, 2).

[155] *Philadelphia,* BDAG 1055.

2. **Philos**, friendship, family love, is mainly concerned with those closest to us.

3. **Stergō** love (which does not appear in the New Testament) is often used for the love and affection between parents and children.

4. "**Agapē** love," expressed by the verb *agapaō*, means "to have a warm regard for and interest in another, cherish, have affection for, love."[156] This is a relatively rare word in Greek, one that Paul essentially defines for the Christian community, a love that is unselfish, caring about the concerns of another person. That is why Paul is sure that "you yourselves have been taught by God to love one another" (4:9b). Unselfish love is rare unless God enables us. "We love because God first loved us" (1 John 4:19).

The Thessalonian church is a loving church. They are known throughout the region for their love for believers. But that doesn't mean that they don't have some growing to do.

I just completed a watercolor painting class at a local community college. The instructor patiently encouraged each student, even though that student's artistic ability had a long way to go before he could be considered competent. The teacher found something good to say about the piece and complemented that. Then she gently encouraged the student in how to improve for the next attempt.

That's what we're seeing here – otherwise Paul wouldn't have mentioned love at all. They are doing well in loving each other, but they still have a ways to go. That is why Paul writes:

"Yet we urge[157] you, brothers, to do so more and more." (1 Thessalonians 4:10b)

"You're doing great," he says, "now keep up the good work." When a child is learning to swing, he or she still needs the parent to push the swing once in a while to keep the momentum going.

Work with Your Own Hands (4:11-12)

The third and final concern Paul writes the Thessalonians about is the idleness that he has observed among them. As we'll see in Lesson 9, there are people in the Christian community who go around from one member to another asking to be fed when they should be working to support themselves. So he says,

---

[156] *Agapaō*, BDAG 5, 1aα.
[157] "Urge" (NIV, NRSV), "beseech" (KJV) is *parakaleō*, "to urge strongly, appeal to, urge, exhort, encourage" (BDAG 765, 2).

> "[11] Make it your ambition[158] to lead a quiet life, to mind your own business and to work with your hands, just as we told you, [12] so that your daily life may win the respect of outsiders and so that you will not be dependent on anybody." (4:11-12)

Paul urges the Thessalonians to live a "quiet" life, that is, a life characterized by peace and orderliness[159] – not out of the proper order of working for a living. As we will see in 2 Thessalonians 3:11, the lazy members were also being "busybodies." So here, Paul tells them to "mind your own business" (NIV), "mind your own affairs" (NRSV), "do your own business" (KJV).[160]

Outsiders aren't impressed when they see lazy Christians sponging off whomever they can. Rather than being lazy, believers must "win the respect" (NIV), "behave properly" (NRSV), "walk honestly" (KJV).[161] Chronic dependency[162] of those who can work is a bad testimony about the transforming power of Jesus Christ.

We'll consider the matter of idleness vs. hard work more thoroughly when we examine 2 Thessalonians 3:6-15 in Lesson 9.

So far, Paul has addressed the church's problems with sexual immorality, love, and chronic dependency. In the next lesson we'll consider Paul's response to this church's misunderstanding about Christ's coming.

Prayer

Father, we live in a world that treats sexual immorality as normal and desirable – as did the world in Paul's day. We need your strength to resist temptation and discipline ourselves. Help us to please you in our sexuality. We pray in Jesus' name. Amen.

---

[158] "Make it your ambition" (NIV), "aspire" (NRSV), "study" (KJV) is *philotimeomai*, "have as one's ambition, consider it an honor, aspire," with focus on idea of rendering service (BDAG 1059). The verb also appears in Romans 15:20 and 2 Corinthians 5:9. A compound verb, literally, "to be fond of honor," but when followed by an infinitive, ""to be ambitious" to, "to strive earnestly, make it one's aim" (Thayer 655, a).

[159] "Lead a quiet life" (NIV), "live quietly" (NRSV), "be quiet" (KJV) is *hēsychazō*, "to live a quiet life or refrain from disturbing activity, be peaceable/orderly" (BDAG 440, 2).

[160] This phrase translates several words. The verb here is *prassō*, "do, accomplish" (BDAG 860, 1a), and the adjective *idios*, "pertaining to a person, through substitution for a pronoun, "own" (BDAG 467, 3a).

[161] The phrase is made up of two words, the verb *paripateō*, "walk, conduct oneself" and the adverb *euschēmonōs*, "pertaining to being proper in behavior, decently, becomingly" (BDAG 414, 1)," in a seemly manner" (Thayer, p. 262).

[162] "Be dependent" (NIV, NRSV), "*that* ye may have lack of nothing" (KJV) uses the verb the verb "to have" with the noun *chreia*, "that which should happen or be supplied because it is needed, need, what should be" (BDAG 1088, 1).

Key Verses

"3 It is God's will that you should be sanctified: that you should avoid sexual immorality; 4 that each of you should learn to control his own body in a way that is holy and honorable, 5 not in passionate lust like the heathen, who do not know God." (1 Thessalonians 4:3-5)

5. The Wonder and Warning of Christ's Return (1 Thessalonians 4:13-5:11)

The Thessalonian church was in turmoil about Christ's return. They expected Jesus to come soon. But since Paul had abruptly left them a year or so before, some of their members have died. Now Timothy reports to Paul a widespread speculation among church members that these newly dead believers would miss out entirely, that Christ's return would be too late for them.

It's fortunate for us that these early Pauline churches had questions and problems. Without them we wouldn't learn so much about Jesus Christ and his wonderful kingdom.

Paul begins this section with a word of comfort and truth to dispel their ignorance and grief.

> "Brothers, we do not want you to be ignorant about those who fall asleep,[163] or to grieve[164] like the rest of men, who have no hope."[165] (4:13)

If you've been to a secular funeral lately, you know the sort of flimsy, "he's-in-a-better-place" sentimentality that bobs hopefully on the surface. But below that, there is no firm expectation of anything beyond this life. And so the grief experienced by the family is deep. They suffer not only the pain of losing someone dear. They have no hope! Praise God! We Christians have a powerful hope!

In this section Paul outlines nine important truths about Christ's coming that should comfort us and prepare us for the future.

1. The Spirits of Sleeping Believers Are with Christ Now (4:14-15)

First, Paul declares some basic Christian beliefs:

> "[14] We believe that Jesus died and rose again and so we believe that God will bring with Jesus those who have fallen asleep in him. [15] According to the Lord's own word, we tell

---

[163] "Fall asleep," of course, is a common Bible metaphor for physical death (Matthew 27:52; John 11:11; Acts 7:60; 13:36; 1 Corinthians 7:39; 11:30; 15:6, 20, 51; 2 Peter 3:4).

[164] "Grieve" (NIV, NRSV), "sorrow" (KJV) is *lypeō*, "be sad, be distressed, grieve" (BDAG 604, 2b).

[165] "Hope" is *elpis*, "the looking forward to something with some reason for confidence respecting fulfillment, hope, expectation" (BDAG 320, 1bβ).

you that we who are still alive, who are left till the coming of the Lord, will certainly not precede those who have fallen asleep." (4:14-15)

We Christians believe:

1. Jesus died,

2. Jesus rose again, and

3. Jesus will return along with the dead in Christ.

If God will "bring[166] with Jesus" the Christian dead, it follows that they are with him now. Hallelujah! Some Christian groups teach "soul sleep," that believers who have died are not in heaven right now. They are in the grave awaiting the resurrection. At that time they will awaken in Christ's presence. So some teach.

However, Paul is pretty clear elsewhere that when he dies, he will instantly be in Christ's presence – and conscious of it!

"I am torn between the two: I desire to depart and be with Christ, which is better by far." (Philippians 1:23)

"Therefore we are always confident and know that as long as we are at home[167] in the body we are away[168] from the Lord. We live by faith, not by sight. We are confident, I say, and would prefer to be away from the body and at home with the Lord." (2 Corinthians 5:6-8)

"He died for us so that, whether we are awake or asleep, we may live together with him." (1 Thessalonians 5:10)

2. The Lord Himself Will Descend from Heaven (4:16)

The second major teaching of this passage is that Christ will return by descending from heaven.

"The Lord himself will come down[169] from heaven, with a loud command, with the voice of the archangel and with the trumpet call of God, and the dead in Christ will rise first." (4:16)

The teaching that Jesus would come in the clouds of heaven begins in Daniel.

"In my vision at night I looked, and there before me was one like a son of man, **coming with the clouds of heaven**. He approached the Ancient of Days and was led into his

---

[166] "Bring" is *agō*, "lead," here, "bring/take along" (BDAG 16, 1b).

[167] *Endēmeō*, "to be in a familiar place, to be at home" (BDAG 332), used in verse 6 and 8 both.

[168] *Ekdēmeō*, "be in a strange land," figuratively, "be away" (BDAG 300), the antonym of *ednēmeō*.

[169] "Come down" (NIV), "descend" (NRSV, KJV) is *katabainō*, "to move downward, come/go/climb down" (BDAG 513,1aγ).

presence. He was given authority, glory and sovereign power; all peoples, nations and men of every language worshiped him. His dominion is an everlasting dominion that will not pass away, and his kingdom is one that will never be destroyed." (Daniel 7:13-14)

Jesus referred to this prophecy several times, so we know that he understood that he was the prophesied Son of Man in this passage. He told his disciples of the events of the Last Days, then announced:

> "At that time men will see the Son of Man **coming in clouds** with great power and glory. And he will send his angels and gather his elect from the four winds, from the ends of the earth to the ends of the heavens." (Mark 13:26-27)

When asked by the high priest at his mock trial if he were the Christ, the Messiah, he answered:

> "I am.... And you will see the Son of Man sitting at the right hand of the Mighty One and **coming on the clouds of heaven**." (Mark 14:62)

The high priest was so upset by this bold statement that he tore his garments. After Jesus' ascension, angels explained:

> "Men of Galilee, why do you stand here looking into the sky? This same Jesus, who has been taken from you into heaven, **will come back in the same way you have seen him go into heaven**." (Acts 1:11)

Finally, in Revelation we read:

> "Look, **he is coming with the clouds**, and every eye will see him, even those who pierced him; and all the peoples of the earth will mourn because of him. So shall it be! Amen." (Revelation 1:7)

Q1. (1 Thessalonians 4:16; Daniel 7:13-14) In what ways does Daniel's prophecy of the Son of Man outline Christ's return? In light of this prophecy, why did Jesus use the title "Son of Man" rather than "Christ" or "Son of God"?
http://www.joyfulheart.com/forums/index.php?showtopic=1231

3. Christ Will Come with Great Glory (4:16)

A third insight regards the glorious manner of Christ's return.

> "The Lord himself will come down from heaven, with a loud command, with the voice
> of the archangel and with the trumpet call of God, and the dead in Christ will rise first."
> (4:16)

When Christ comes, it won't be secretly (as some teach with no Scriptural support) or quietly. When he returns he will come with great glory. Notice these elements:

a. Loud command. This phrase translated "loud command" (NIV), "cry of command" (NRSV), "shout" (KJV) is *keleusma*, "signal, (cry of) command," from *keleuō*, "to order, command (military command)."[170] When Christ returns he will come with a Conqueror's command.

b. Voice of the archangel (*archangelos*), "a member of the higher ranks in the celestial hierarchy, chief angel, archangel."[171] Michael is mentioned as an archangel in Jude 9.

c. Trumpet call.[172] Trumpets were used in battle, like a bugle in the American Civil War, to signal war commands. They were also used to announce rulers and great events. This trumpet call is mentioned elsewhere:

> "In that day **a great trumpet will sound**. Those who were perishing in Assyria and those
> who were exiled in Egypt will come and worship the LORD on the holy mountain in
> Jerusalem." (Isaiah 27:13)

> "And he will send his angels with a **loud trumpet call**, and they will gather his elect
> from the four winds, from one end of the heavens to the other." (Matthew 24:31)

> "Listen, I tell you a mystery: We will not all sleep, but we will all be changed – in a flash,
> in the twinkling of an eye, **at the last trumpet**. For the **trumpet will sound**, the dead will
> be raised imperishable, and we will be changed." (1 Corinthians 15:51-52)

4. Christ Will Come with All His Holy Ones (4:14)

Fourth, Christ will come with all the saints who have died previously – and with an army of angels.

> "We believe that Jesus died and rose again and so we believe that God will **bring with
> Jesus those who have fallen asleep in him**." (4:14)

We saw this verse under point 1 above, but I want to explain its significance here. Many Old Testament prophecies will be fulfilled at this time. Those who have died in

---

[170] *Keleusma*, BDAG 538.

[171] *Archangelos*, BDAG 132. Our English words "archangel," "archenemy," and "archbishop" all use the Greek prefix *arch-*, "chief, leader, ruler."

[172] "Trumpet call" (NIV), "sound of God's trumpet" (NRSV), "trump" (KJV) is *salpinx*, "a wind instrument used especially for communication, trumpet," then the sound made or signal given by a trumpet, trumpet-call, trumpet-sound" (BDAG 912, 2).

Christ are with him now. But when he comes, they will come with him, like a mighty army of the saints in the company of the Returning King, along with myriad angels.

> "Then the LORD my God will come, and **all the holy ones with him**." (Zechariah 14:5b)

> "When the Son of Man comes in his glory, **and all the angels with him**, he will sit on his throne in heavenly glory." (Matthew 25:31)

> "Enoch, the seventh from Adam, prophesied about these men: 'See, the Lord is coming **with thousands upon thousands of his holy ones**.'" (Jude 14, quoting 1 Enoch 1:9)

It will be a glorious Day!

On that day, when Christ brings with him those who have died in Christ, their bodies will be resurrected and reunited with their spirits. Look at this verse again alongside 1 Corinthians 15:51-52:

> "[14] We believe that Jesus died and rose again and so we believe that **God will bring with Jesus those who have fallen asleep in him**. [15] According to the Lord's own word, we tell you that we who are still alive, who are left[173] till the coming of the Lord, will certainly not precede[174] those who have fallen asleep." (4:14-15)

> "Listen, I tell you a mystery: We will not all sleep, but we will all be changed – in a flash, in the twinkling of an eye, at the last trumpet. For the trumpet will sound, **the dead will be raised imperishable**, and we will be changed." (1 Corinthians 15:51-52)

Blind songwriter Fanny Crosby wrote a song, "In the Twinkling of an Eye" (1898) that explains this truth:

> "When He comes in the clouds descending,
> And they who loved Him here,
> From their graves shall awake and praise Him
> With joy and not with fear;
> **When the body and the soul are united**,
> And clothed no more to die,
> What a shouting there will be
> When each other's face we see,
> Changed in the twinkling of an eye."

Imagine standing in a graveyard watching this great meeting unfold!

---

[173] "Are left" (NIV, NRSV), "remain" (KJV) is *perileipomai*, "remain, be left behind," both here and in verse 17 (BDAG 802).

[174] "Precede" (NIV, NRSV), "prevent" (KJV) is *phthanō*, "to be beforehand in moving to a position, come before, precede" (BDAG 1053, 1). "Prevent" (KJV) is an archaic usage which means, "to go or arrive before," from Latin *praeventus*, from *prae-* "before" + *venire*, "to come."

Q2. (1 Thessalonians 4:14) How will Christ bring with him those believers who have previously died? According to Matthew 25:31, who will also will accompany Christ when he returns?

http://www.joyfulheart.com/forums/index.php?showtopic=1232

They are with him now —
angles will also acompany him

5. Christ Will Gather All His People Together in the Rapture (4:17)

Fifth, not only will the dead in Christ come with him, be raised from the dead, and reunited with their bodies, but all Christians still alive on the earth will be caught up to be with him also.

> "After that, we who are still alive and are left will be caught up together with them in the clouds to meet the Lord in the air. And so we will be with the Lord forever." (4:17)

This event is popularly known as "the rapture." The Greek word translated "caught up" is *harpazō*, "snatch, seize", that is, "take suddenly and vehemently, or take away." Here, "to grab or seize suddenly so as to remove or gain control, snatch/take away."[175] In Latin the word is *raptus* ("seized") from which we get our word "rapture."[176]

This, too, will fulfill many Old Testament prophecies. After the exile of the Northern Kingdom to Assyria (729 BC) and the Southern Kingdom to Babylon (604 BC to 587 BC), there was grief that God's people would never be reunited. But the prophets foresaw that, indeed, all Israel would be gathered together on the Day of the Lord.

> "He will raise a banner for the nations and **gather** the exiles of Israel; he will **assemble** the scattered people of Judah **from the four quarters of the earth**." (Isaiah 11:12)

> "'Lift up your eyes and look around; all your sons **gather** and come to you. As surely as I live,' declares the LORD, 'you will wear them all as ornaments; you will put them on, like a bride.'" (Isaiah 49:18)

> "Lift up your eyes and look about you: **All assemble** and come to you; your sons come from afar, and your daughters are carried on the arm." (Isaiah 60:4)

This sounds much like the wording of Jesus' prophecy concerning this "gathering."

---

[175] *Harpazō*, BDAG 134, 2b.
[176] "Rape" (from Latin *rapere*) used to mean "to seize and take away by force," then "to despoil."

"And he will send out his angels with a loud trumpet call, and they will **gather**[177] his elect **from the four winds**, from one end of heaven to the other." (Matthew 24:31 ‖ Mark 13:27)

In 2 Thessalonians, we see this same language regarding the rapture.[178]

"Concerning the coming of our Lord Jesus Christ and our **being gathered**[179] to him...." (2 Thessalonians 2:1)

The resurrection of the dead and the rapture are closely linked by Paul, and seem to occur nearly simultaneously. It is designed to comfort the grieving Thessalonians:

"Therefore encourage each other with these words." (4:18)

6. The Day of the Lord Will Come Suddenly (5:1-3)

Paul's teaching regarding Christ's second coming continues with a sixth point, that there will be no further warning. Christ will come suddenly. We may know the general season of his coming (Matthew 24:32-33), but not the exact time (Matthew 24:36; Mark 13:32; Acts 1:7).

"[1] Now concerning the times and the seasons, brothers and sisters, you do not need to have anything written to you. [2] For you yourselves know very well that the day of the Lord will come like a thief in the night." (5:1-2)

When he was with the Thessalonian Christians, Paul had taught them that Jesus would come "like a thief in the night," that is, unexpectedly and without notice. He is recalling Jesus' own teaching regarding the abruptness of his coming.

"Therefore keep watch, because you do not know on what day your Lord will come. But understand this: If the owner of the house had known at what time of night the **thief** was coming, he would have kept watch and would not have let his house be broken into. So you also must be ready, because **the Son of Man will come at an hour when you do not expect him**." (Matthew 24:42-44)

We see the same phrase in 2 Peter and Revelation. This was the clear apostolic tradition. Jesus would come suddenly.

"But the day of the Lord will **come like a thief**." (2 Peter 3:10a)

---

[177] "Gather" is *episynagō*, "to bring together, gather (together)" (BDAG 382).

[178] We even see what may be a symbolic hint of the rapture in Revelation regarding the "two witnesses": "Then they heard a loud voice from heaven saying to them, 'Come up here.' And they went up to heaven in a cloud, while their enemies looked on" (Revelation 11:12). Of course, this is a difficult passage to interpret.

[179] "Gathered" is *episynagōgē*, "the action of assembling" (BDAG 382, 2).

> "If you do not wake up, I will **come like a thief**, and you will not know at what time I will come to you." (Revelation 3:3b)

> "Behold, I **come like a thief**! Blessed is he who stays awake and keeps his clothes with him, so that he may not go naked and be shamefully exposed." (Revelation 16:15)

7. Christ's Coming Will Bring Sudden Judgment and Destruction upon the Wicked (5:3)

Now Paul continues to spell out the implications of Christ's sudden return in his seventh point.

> "When they say, 'There is peace and security,' then **sudden destruction** will come upon them, as labor pains come upon a pregnant woman, and there will be no escape!" (5:3)

People will be commenting on how peaceful it is, when Christ will suddenly come with judgment and the wrath of God against wickedness.[180] Christ's coming won't necessarily be immediately preceded by war and turmoil (Matthew 24:6). Paul compares Christ's coming with the sudden onset of labor pains. At that point it will be too late to get ready. The time is upon us! Jesus had taught the same thing, using the analogies of Noah and Sodom from Genesis.

> "Just as it was **in the days of Noah**, so too it will be in the days of the Son of Man. They were eating and drinking, and marrying and being given in marriage, until the day Noah entered the ark, and the flood came and destroyed all of them. Likewise, just as it was **in the days of Lot**: they were eating and drinking, buying and selling, planting and building, but on the day that Lot left Sodom, it rained fire and sulfur from heaven and destroyed all of them." (Luke 17:26-29)

I don't want to refer to all the terrible prophecies of this judgment, especially in the Book of Revelation. They are frightening. But here is a sample.

> "The day of the Lord will come like a thief, and then the heavens will pass away with a loud noise, and the elements will be dissolved with fire, and the earth and everything that is done on it will be disclosed." (2 Peter 3:10)

The Day of Christ's Coming will be awesome in its swiftness, its glory, and its judgment.

Q3. (1 Thessalonians 5:1-3) According to this passage, what warning can we expect to have prior to Christ's return? What does it mean that he will "come like a thief"?
http://www.joyfulheart.com/forums/index.php?showtopic=1233

---

[180] A number of New Testament Scriptures talk about God's wrath upon the wicked on the Last Day (Matthew 3:7; Colossians 3:6; 2 Peter 2:9-10; Revelation 6:16-17; 11:18; 14:19; 15:1, 7; 16:1, 19; 19:15).

8. In Light of Christ's Coming We Must Remain Awake and Self-Controlled (5:4-8)

The eighth point in Paul's explanation of Christ's coming moves to the *effect* that such knowledge should have on us as believers.

> "⁴ But you, brothers, are not in darkness so that this day should surprise you like a thief. ⁵ You are all sons of the light and sons of the day.[181] We do not belong to the night or to the darkness. ⁶ So then, let us not be like others, who are asleep, but **let us be alert and self-controlled.** ⁷ For those who sleep, sleep at night, and those who get drunk, get drunk at night. ⁸ But since we belong to the day, **let us be self-controlled, putting on faith and love** as a breastplate, and the **hope** of salvation as a helmet." (5:4-8)

The believers may be frightened now, but Paul consoles them by reminding them that they are not the targets of Christ's judgment, but rather the ones he died to save. He does, however, give them a command:

> "So then ... let us be alert and self-controlled." (5:6)

a. Be Sober, Self-Controlled

Paul commands the Thessalonians to be "self-controlled" (NIV), "sober" (NRSV, KJV). *Nēphō* originally meant "be sober." In the New Testament it is used figuratively: "to be free from every form of mental and spiritual 'drunkenness', from excess, passion, rashness, confusion, etc., be well-balanced, self-controlled."[182] "To be calm and collected in spirit; to be temperate, dispassionate, circumspect."[183] Jesus, too, used the context of his coming to warn his disciples against profligacy in his Parable of the Wise and Faithful Servant:

> "But suppose that servant is wicked and says to himself, 'My master is staying away a long time,' and he then begins to beat his fellow servants and to eat and drink with drunkards. The master of that servant will come on a day when he does not expect him and at an hour he is not aware of. He will cut him to pieces and assign him a place with the hypocrites, where there will be weeping and gnashing of teeth." (Matthew 24:48-51)

Belief in Christ's soon coming should cause us to watch our behavior.

b. Be Alert

Paul also commands the believers to "be alert" (NIV), "stay awake" (NRSV), "watch" (KJV). The verb is *grēgoreō*, with the basic meaning of literally "to stay awake, be

---

[181] "Put your trust in the light while you have it, so that you may become sons of light" (John 12:36a). "For you were once darkness, but now you are light in the Lord. Live as children of light" (Ephesians 5:8).

[182] *Nēphō*, BDAG 672.

[183] *Nēphō*, Thayer 425.

watchful." Here Paul is using the word figuratively: "to be in constant readiness, be on the alert" (similar to our, 'Keep your eyes open').[184] "Be vigilant."[185]

Jesus used this idea in two parables about the last days – the Parable of the Ten Virgins and the Parable of the Watchful Servant:

> "The bridegroom was a long time in coming, and they all became drowsy and fell asleep.... **Keep awake** therefore, for you know neither the day nor the hour." (Matthew 25:5, 13)

> "Be on guard! Be alert! You do not know when that time will come.... Therefore **keep watch** because you do not know when the owner of the house will come back – whether in the evening, or at midnight, or when the rooster crows, or at dawn. If he comes suddenly, do not let him find you sleeping. What I say to you, I say to everyone: **'Watch!'**" (Mark 13:33, 35-37)

You see this kind of exhortation again and again in the New Testament epistles:

> "**Be on your guard**; stand firm in the faith; be men of courage; be strong." (1 Corinthians 16:13)

> "**Be alert** and always keep on praying for all the saints." (Ephesians 6:18b)

> "Devote yourselves to prayer, **being watchful** and thankful." (Colossians 4:2)

> "Therefore, **prepare your minds for action; be self-controlled**...." (1 Peter 1:13)

> "The end of all things is near. Therefore **be clear minded and self-controlled** so that you can pray." (1 Peter 4:7)

> "**Be self-controlled and alert**. Your enemy the devil prowls around like a roaring lion looking for someone to devour." (1 Peter 5:8)

> "**Wake up**! Strengthen what remains." (Revelation 3:2, to the Church at Sardis)

> "Behold, I come like a thief! **Blessed is he who stays awake**...." (Revelation 16:15)

My friend, are you awake spiritually, or apathetic and inactive in the Lord's work? Are you exercising self-control? Are you ready for Christ's coming?

Paul tells us how to prepare yourselves:

> "**... Putting on faith and love** as a breastplate, and the **hope** of salvation as a helmet." (1 Thessalonians 5:8b)

This sounds a lot like Paul's trinity of virtues in 1 Corinthians 13:

> "And now these three remain: faith, hope and love. But the greatest of these is love." (1 Corinthians 13:13)

---

[184] *Grēgoreō*, BDAG 208, 2.
[185] Albrecht Oepke, *egeirō*, TDNT 2:333-339. "To be or become fully awake, watch" (Liddell-Scott).

Notice how Paul uses analogies that suggest equipping oneself for battle. It is reminiscent of teachings to other churches about the "full armor of God" (Ephesians 6:11-18), "the armor of light" (Romans 13:12), and "weapons of righteousness" (2 Corinthians 6:7). To be alert and self-controlled requires positive efforts to take hold of God's spiritual resources at all times.

Q4. (1 Thessalonians 5:4-8) What effect should a belief in Christ's soon coming have on believers? What does it mean to be "sober" or "self-controlled" (verse 6)? What does it mean to be "alert" or "watchful" (verse 6)? How does this differ from our normal Christian lifestyle?

http://www.joyfulheart.com/forums/index.php?showtopic=1234

9. Believers Are Destined for Salvation, not Wrath (5:9)

Paul concludes this teaching, intended to comfort the confused believers, with an ninth point. They are not the intended recipients of the wrath of God when Christ comes – similar to what we read in 1:10.

> "... To wait for his Son from heaven, whom he raised from the dead – Jesus, who rescues us from the coming wrath." (1 Thessalonians 1:10)

> "For God did not appoint[186] us to suffer wrath but to receive salvation through our Lord Jesus Christ. [10] He died for us so that, whether we are awake or asleep, we may live together with him." (5:9-10)

Some teachers try to use 5:9 to "prove" that true Christians won't go through the tribulation. They believe that Christ will come (secretly) – before the tribulation (pre-trib) – and take the true Christians up in the rapture. I disagree. Because this has been a popular view among evangelical Christians, I'll make a couple of points. But this isn't

---

[186] "Appoint" (NIV, KJV), "destined" (NRSV) is the very common verb *tithēmi*, "to put, place," here, in the middle voice with a double accusative, "consign someone to something" (BDAG 1003, 5b). The thought of 5:9 is similar to Acts 13:48, which says, "When the Gentiles heard this, they were glad and honored the word of the Lord; and all who were appointed for eternal life believed. Acts 13:48. "Appointed" (NIV), "destined" (NRSV), "ordained" (KJV) as in Acts 13:48 is *tassō*, "arrange, put in place," here, "assign someone to a (certain) classification" (BDAG 992, 1b).

the place for a full debate of the pre-trib rapture.[187] If we disagree about this, I'll still love you and you'll love me.

1. **Wrath**. 1 Thessalonians 5:9 says that God didn't consign us to the wrathful judgment of God, but to salvation. It does *not* say that Christians won't go through at least part of the Great Tribulation (during a time when some unbelievers are feeling the effects of God's wrath).

2. **Scripture**. A number of scriptures indicate that some Christians will go through at least some of the tribulation (Matthew 24:9-14, 21-22, 29-31; 1 Thessalonians 3:2-4; Revelation 7:2-8, 9-14; 13:10; 14:12).

I know that proponents have an answer for each objection. I'm just not convinced by their arguments for a secret rapture prior to the tribulation – especially since it requires a *speculative harmonization* of a number of verses interpreted in a certain specific way. The pre-trib rapture itself is nowhere taught in Scripture.

Our verse, however, assures us that the coming wrath is not our destiny. Our destiny is salvation and eternal life through Jesus Christ our Lord. Hallelujah! Paul reminds us:

> "He died for us so that, whether we are awake or asleep, we may live together with him." (5:10)

Our loved ones who have died in Christ are safe and saved. They will be present to witness and participate in Christ's great coming.

Summary (5:11)

Paul had taught them about Christ's Second Coming previously. But in this passage he has outlined nine important points to comfort the grieving believers in Thessalonica – and us!

Here are those nine points for review:

1. The spirits of sleeping believers are with Christ now (4:14-15; 5:9).

2. The Lord himself will descend from heaven (4:16).

3. Christ will come with great glory (4:16).

---

[187] I've studied this issue from all angles and just don't find the Dispensational arguments convincing. To believe in the pre-trib rapture I'd have to believe a number of interpretations of Scripture that I'm just not comfortable with. For more on this see a popular-level discussion in Marvin Rosenthal, *The Pre-Wrath Rapture of the Church* (Nelson, 1990) and my study, *The Book of Revelation: Discipleship Lessons* (JesusWalk Publications, 2004, 2011). The pre-trib view is relatively new in Church history in the 1830s by John Nelson Darby and the Plymouth Brethren, and popularized in the US in the early 20th century through the Scofield Reference Bible and the Bible School Movement.

4. Christ will come with all his holy ones (4:14).

5. Christ will gather all his people together in the rapture (4:17).

6. The day of the Lord will come suddenly (5:1-3).

7. Christ's coming will bring sudden judgment and destruction upon the wicked (5:3).

8. In light of Christ's coming we must remain awake and self-controlled (5:4-8).

9. Believers are destined for salvation, not wrath (5:9).

Paul concludes this section:

> "Therefore encourage one another and build each other up, just as in fact you are doing." (5:11)

Prayer

Thank you, Father, for the promise of Christ's coming. We ask you to hasten the day and help us to be ready. We also ask you to send a mighty revival so that as many as possible might come to know you before the end comes and it is too late. In Jesus' mighty name, we pray. Amen.

Key Verses

> "We believe that Jesus died and rose again and so we believe that God will bring with Jesus those who have fallen asleep in him." (1 Thessalonians 4:14)

> "For the Lord himself will come down from heaven, with a loud command, with the voice of the archangel and with the trumpet call of God, and the dead in Christ will rise first. After that, we who are still alive and are left will be caught up together with them in the clouds to meet the Lord in the air. And so we will be with the Lord forever." (1 Thessalonians 4:16-17)

Faithful Ministry (5:14)

> "And we urge you, brothers, warn those who are idle, encourage the timid, help the weak, be patient with everyone." (5:14)

Now Paul speaks to the church in general. The pronoun "you" and the word "beloved" or "brothers" are in the plural. Note that the plural of "brothers," *adelphoi*, can refer to both "brothers and sisters," as the NRSV indicates. In verse 12, Paul referred to the role of leaders to admonish the church. Now he is more specific about the general approach to shepherding needed in Thessalonica. Verse 14 could even be a four-part guideline for pastoral ministry:

1. Admonish the idle. "Those who are idle" (NIV), "idlers" (NRSV), "them that are unruly" (KJV) is the adjective *ataktos*, which means, "not in the proper order." It is sometimes used of soldiers who are out of the ranks. Here it is used in the sense of "being out of step and going one's own way, disorderly, insubordinate," though some prefer the sense "idle, indolent."[195] Paul uses the adverb of this root (*ataktōs*) in 2 Thessalonians 3:6, where the context is people who don't work but are dependent upon others. So "idlers" is probably a more useful translation of what Paul was referring to in our verse. He had admonished them concerning idleness in 4:11-12. Perhaps "idlers" could be applied to the way people behave in church, too. Some people come to church only to be served, not to serve. They are takers, not givers. Everyone has at least one spiritual gift. It's the role of leaders to "admonish the idle," both in physical things and in spiritual ministry.

2. Encourage the timid.[196] The church has been suffering persecution, and some need to be encouraged to stand up rather than hunker down in order to avoid any criticism or persecution.

3. Help[197] **the weak.**[198] The weak referred to in light of persecution are probably those who are weak in faith, though the principle would apply to those who are ill or weak in

---

[195] *Ataktos*, BDAG 148, 1; Thayer 83.

[196] "Timid" (NIV), "fainthearted" (NRSV), "feebleminded" (KJV) is *oligopsychos*, "faint-hearted, discouraged" (BDAG 703), from *oligos*, "little, small" + *psychē*, "souled." The related verb *oligopseucheō* occurs in the ancient papyri. Robertson comments, "Local conditions often cause some to lose heart and wish to drop out, be quitters. These must be held in line." (Robertson, *Word Pictures*). "Encourage" (NIV, NRSV), "comfort" is *paramytheomai*, "console, cheer up," especially in connection with death or other tragic events. (BDAG 769).

[197] "Help" (NIV, NRSV), "support" (KJV) is *antechō*, "to have strong interest in, hence help someone or something" (BDAG 87, 2).

[198] "Weak" is *asthenēs*, of that which lacks strength, "weak, powerless." The word is sometimes used of the sick.

other ways. The church is to encourage them and lift up their hands. Though we're not to help in such a way that we encourage an unhealthy dependence (4:11-12). Leaders often visit the sick, or encourage those with a special ministry to the sick to visit them.

4. Be patient with everyone. "Patient" is *makrothymeō*, "to bear up under provocation without complaint, be patient, forbearing."[199] Leaders, especially, must learn to be even tempered, even with those who don't deserve it. Make allowances for those who haven't grown in Christ as much as they should. Parents learn patience; so must church leaders.

Kind, Not Vengeful (5:15)

One mark of a healthy congregation is the absence of a judgmental spirit. In many churches, unfortunately, you sense a kind of spiritual pride in their own righteousness, and a condescending attitude towards those who are not as spiritual, or even outright secular. Our attitude reflects rather accurately how well we've matured in incorporating *agapē* love into our church life.

Part of this kind of non-judgmental, open love, is the absence of vengefulness -- a childish desire to get even.

> "Make sure that nobody pays back[200] wrong for wrong, but always try to be kind[201] to each other and to everyone else." (5:15)

To the Roman church, Paul writes on this topic more expansively.

> "[17] Do not repay anyone evil for evil. Be careful to do what is right in the eyes of everybody. [18] If it is possible, as far as it depends on you, live at peace with everyone. [19] Do not take revenge, my friends, but leave room for God's wrath, for it is written: 'It is mine to avenge; I will repay,' says the Lord. [20] On the contrary: 'If your enemy is hungry, feed him; if he is thirsty, give him something to drink. In doing this, you will heap burning coals on his head.' [21] Do not be overcome by evil, but overcome evil with good." (Romans 12:17-21)

Peter, too, commands the same kind of loving behavior when provoked.

> "Do not repay evil with evil or insult with insult, but with blessing, because to this you were called so that you may inherit a blessing." (1 Peter 3:9)

---

[199] *Makrothymeō*, BDAG 612, 2.

[200] "Pays back" (NIV), "repays" (NRSV), "render" (KJV) is *apodidōmi*, "to recompense, whether in a good or bad sense, render, reward, recompense" (BDAG 110, 4).

[201] "Be kind" (NIV), "do good" (NRSV), "follow that which is good" (KJV) is two words, agathos, "good" and *diōkō*, which has the basic idea of "cause to flee." It can mean, "to persecute," but here it is used in a positive sense, "be in haste in order to find something, run after, pursue," figuratively, "strive for, seek after, aspire to something" (BDAG 254, 4b).

Jesus was very clear that his followers must be forgiving (Matthew 6:12, 14-15; 18:23-35). People who must pay back every hurt are miserable, selfish, vengeful wrecks, not healthy Christians who take their cues from Christ himself.

Q2. (1 Thessalonians 5:15) What happens to people who seek revenge on those who hurt them? What happens when they neglect to forgive those who have wronged them? What happens in a congregation that has an unloving, superior attitude towards outsiders? How do these attitudes reflect on Christ? How can people or congregations get healthy after have been vengeful, proud, or unforgiving?
http://www.joyfulheart.com/forums/index.php?showtopic=1236

Be Joyful, Prayerful, and Thankful (5:16-18)

The next key to a healthy congregation – and personal life – is spiritual enthusiasm. In this memorable passage, Paul commands,

> "[16] Be joyful always; [17] pray continually; [18] give thanks in all circumstances, for this is God's will for you in Christ Jesus." (5:16-18)

It almost sounds like a surface platitude until you begin to think about what Paul is saying.

Be Joyful Always (5:16)

"Be joyful[202] always" (NIV), "rejoice always" (NRSV), "rejoice evermore" (KJV) is a command to rejoice. This is not the same as a command to "be happy in spite of yourself." Or to "put on a good face." It is a command to continue to praise God and enjoy the presence of God, even when circumstances around you are adverse. When we stop finding joy in God, that means that our faith has been distracted and our focus has shifted from God to wallowing in our circumstances. Paul tells the Philippians:

> "Rejoice in the Lord always. I will say it again: Rejoice!" (Philippians 4:4)

---

[202] "Be joyful" (NIV), "rejoice" (NRSV, KJV) is *chairō*, "to be in a state of happiness and well-being, rejoice, be glad" (BDAG 1074, 1).

We are to rejoice always, all the time.[203] This means that putting our focus on God and finding joy in him is to be a continual life habit and pattern. Developing a practice of continual rejoicing is a worthy goal for your spiritual growth.

Pray Continually (5:17)

Pray continually![204] Some strands of the Eastern Orthodox Church seek to fulfill this command by repeating the "Jesus Prayer" thousands of times a day, again and again by rote until it is engrained in the mind.[205] But Paul's command doesn't mean mumbling prayers without stop during all our waking hours. It means that prayer should be an integral part of our lives, that we are constantly turning to prayer, rather than forgetting about talking to God for days at a time. Look at Paul's practice in this letter and elsewhere:

> "We **always** thank God for all of you, mentioning you in our prayers. We **continually** remember before our God and Father...." (1:2-3)

> "And we also thank God **continually** because...." (2:13)

> "**Night and day** we pray most earnestly that...." (3:10)

> "God ... is my witness how **constantly** I remember you in my prayers at all times...." (Romans 1:9-10)

> "I **have not stopped** giving thanks for you, remembering you in my prayers." (Ephesians 1:16)

> "Pray in the Spirit **on all occasions** with all kinds of prayers and requests. With this in mind, be alert and **always keep on** praying for all the saints." (Ephesians 6:18)

> "We **have not stopped** praying for you and asking God to...." (Colossians 1:9)

> "**Devote** yourselves to prayer, being watchful and thankful." (Colossians 4:2)

The conclusion I reach is that continual prayer is the spiritual practice of shooting up prayers to God constantly – perhaps every few minutes as you think of something to pray about. God wants us to learn a life of prayer, of talking to God constantly about whatever is going on in our lives, or about the thoughts he brings to our minds. Pray continually!

---

[203] "Always" (NIV, NRSV), "evermore" (KJV) is the common adverb *pantote*, "always, at all times" (BDAG 755).

[204] The word "continually" (NIV), "without ceasing" (NRSV, KJV) is *adialeiptōs*, "constantly, unceasingly" (BDAG 20).

[205] For example, Anthony M. Coniaris, *A Beginner's Introduction to the Philokalia* (Minneapolis: Light and Life Publishing Company, 2004), pp. 48-53; Helen Bacovcin (translator), *The Way of a Pilgrim and The Pilgrim Continues His Way* (Doubleday, 1978).

Give Thanks in All Circumstances (5:18a)

"Give thanks" is *eucharisteō*, "to express appreciation for benefits or blessings, give thanks, express thanks, render/return thanks."[206] There's a key insight in Paul's letter to the Philippian church:

> "Do not be anxious about anything, but in everything, by prayer and petition, **with thanksgiving**, present your requests to God." (Philippians 4:6)

So often we pray whining prayers, complaining, begging prayers, pleading prayers. What would happen if we started praying prayers filled with thanksgiving? What separates whining prayers from faith-filled prayers is thanksgiving. Thanksgiving turns us to look at all the times God has helped us in the past, his unchanging character, his marvelous promises – and to thank God for them. We can't do that without increasing our faith. Thanksgiving is the language of faith.

Paul says to "give thanks in all circumstances."[207] Notice that it does not say, "thank God *for* all circumstances," but *"in* all circumstances." Sometimes we are in the midst of an evil attack. I think it's stupid to pray, "Thank you God that Satan is attacking me and causing me to be raped." We're not thankful for evil. But in the midst of evil we can give thanks to God for his sovereignty, for his power, for his presence, and for his final victory over evil. We win – so we should always give thanks no matter what is going on.

This Is God's Will for You in Christ Jesus (5:18b)

What is God's will for you right now? At the moment you may not know what the future holds or the answer to some crucial decision you need to make. But you can be sure about one thing – how God wants you to act in the circumstances in which you find yourself.

> "Be joyful always; pray continually; give thanks in all circumstances, for this is God's will for you in Christ Jesus." (5:16-18)

Imagine what would happen if you – or the people in your congregation – were to put this into practice consistently. You'd grow healthy fast!

Q3. (1 Thessalonians 5:16-18) In your own words explain how a person can rejoice and pray continually. Are there any circumstances we might be in the midst of where we

---

[206] *Eucharisteō*, BDAG 415, 2.

[207] "In all circumstances" (NIV, NRSV), "in everything" (KJV) is two words, the preposition *en*, "in" and the extremely common adjective *pas*, "all, everything," here, probably, with the sense of, "everything belonging, in kind, to the class designated by the noun, every kind of, all sorts of" (BDAG 784, 5).

should not give thanks to God?

http://www.joyfulheart.com/forums/index.php?showtopic=1237

Don't Quench the Spirit, but Test Prophetic Words (5:19-22)

Paul is sharing brief instructions as he concludes this letter. Here's one that leads to congregational health.

> "[19] Do not put out[208] the Spirit's fire; [20] do not treat prophecies with contempt. [21] Test everything. Hold on to the good. [22] Avoid every kind of evil." (5:19-22)

John the Baptist said that Jesus would baptize "with the Holy Spirit and with fire" (Luke 3:16b). The Spirit is a fire. He cannot be controlled or domesticated by us. When we try to restrain him or pour cold water over him and his working, we err.

Apparently, the Thessalonian church had had some bad experiences with people in the congregation prophesying things that didn't occur or that were doctrinally incorrect. They may have gotten to the point that when someone prophesied in the congregation, there was a negative feeling. Prophecies weren't appreciated, perhaps not allowed at all.

"Treat with contempt" (NIV), "despise" (NRSV, KJV) is *exoutheneō*, "to show by one's attitude or manner of treatment that an entity has no merit or worth, disdain." Here, probably, "to have no use for something as being beneath one's consideration, reject disdainfully."[209] When we begin to despise that true working of God through the Spirit because of our prejudices and doctrines, we're in the same danger as the Pharisees who wanted to destroy Jesus for healing on the Sabbath.

Prophecy in the Corinthian Church (1 Corinthians 14)

A careful study of 1 Corinthians 14 could be useful here. I'll just hit the highlights. The Corinthian church valued speaking in tongues, but didn't value prophecy very much, though both were utterances by the Spirit. In practice, the Corinthians were speaking in tongues out loud in a church gathering without interpretation, at the same time as they neglected the much more versatile and upbuilding gift of prophecy.

---

[208] "Put out fire" (NIV), "quench" (NRSV, KJV) is *sbennymi*, "to cause an action, state, or faculty to cease to function or exist, quench, put out." It can be used literally of fire, "extinguish." Here it is used figuratively, "quench, stifle, suppress" (*Sbennymi*, BDAG 917, b).

[209] *Exoutheneō*, BDAG 352, 2.

> "He who speaks in a tongue edifies himself, but he who prophesies edifies the church. I would like every one of you to speak in tongues, but I would rather have you prophesy. He who prophesies is greater than one who speaks in tongues, unless he interprets, so that the church may be edified." (1 Corinthians 14:4-5)

As I have explained elsewhere,[210] prophecy in this context isn't the same as inspired preaching (though occasionally I've heard true prophecy in the midst of a sermon). Prophecy is the Holy Spirit speaking directly to the congregation through the mouth of a gifted believer. Prophecy, when it comes from the Holy Spirit, edifies or builds up the church. Prophecy can sometimes speak directly to an unbeliever who might be present and result in his salvation (1 Corinthians 14:24-25).

Paul includes prophecy as one element of the regular meeting of the church, here referred to as a "revelation."

> "When you come together, everyone has a hymn, or a word of instruction, a revelation, a tongue or an interpretation. All of these must be done for the strengthening of the church." (1 Corinthians 14:26)

Apparently people were interrupting each other and acting as if they couldn't control themselves, with the result that the service was disorderly (a problem that some churches have in our day). So Paul gives instructions so that prophecy can be given and evaluated in an orderly manner.

> "Two or three prophets should speak, and the others should weigh carefully what is said. And if a revelation comes to someone who is sitting down, the first speaker should stop. For you can all prophesy in turn so that everyone may be instructed and encouraged. The spirits of prophets are subject to the control of prophets. For God is not a God of disorder but of peace." (1 Corinthians 14:29-33a)

Notice that even when the Holy Spirit comes upon a prophet to prophecy, he or she can wait for the appropriate time to give the prophecy. It isn't a compulsive gift (though sometimes people without much experience with tongues or prophecy don't understand this). Note well that everything prophesied should *not* be taken as the "gospel truth."

> "Two or three prophets should speak, and the others should weigh carefully[211] what is said." (1 Corinthians 14:29)

---

[210] See my article, "Understanding the Gift of Prophecy. I. Is Prophecy Preaching?" www.joyfulheart.com/scholar/preach.htm

[211] "Weigh carefully" (NIV), "weigh" (NRSV), "judge" (KJV) is *diakrinō*, "separate, differentiate, here figuratively, "to evaluate by paying careful attention to, evaluate, judge" (BDAG 233, 3a).

Test Prophecies (5:21-22)

This is the same thing that Paul is saying to the Thessalonian church:

> "21 Test everything. Hold on to the good. 22 Avoid every kind of evil." (1 Thessalonians 5:21-22)

This word "test" (NIV), "prove" (KJV) is *dokimazō*, which we saw in 2:4: "to make a critical examination of something to determine genuineness, put to the test, examine."[212] In other words, when a prophecy is given, there should be a time of reflection. Perhaps some of the more mature Christians might comment on what God might be speaking to the group, how it fits (or doesn't fit) the Scripture. Instead of rejecting prophecy out of hand (as many churches do today), the group needs to reflect on it. Not everything that comes as a prophecy is pure from God. It goes through a human filter that sometimes introduces error. We need to be discerning.

It's also important to realize that prophecy doesn't trump or replace the Scripture. It is not at the same level. Prophecies are judged by Scripture. They should not replace the Scriptures or become an authoritative appendix for doctrine.[213]

But it is also important not to despise prophesying, as many churches do today. Let's get it right. We're open to the Spirit. We allow prophecy. But we don't adopt it as from God until we take time to reflect on it, test it by scripture, and make sure it doesn't lead us astray. When we find it to be from God, then we should "hold on to" it.[214] If, on the other hand, a prophecy contains error or evil, we should keep away from it.[215]

Q4. (1 Thessalonians 5:19-22; 1 Corinthians 14) Why do churches sometimes despise or prohibit prophecy? What guidelines does Paul give here and in 1 Corinthians 14 to keep prophecy in a congregation healthy?

http://www.joyfulheart.com/forums/index.php?showtopic=1238

---

[212] *Dokimazō*, BDAG 256, 1.

[213] I can think of two prominent groups that seem to have exalted prophecies and revelations inappropriately – the Seventh Day Adventists, with the writings of their founder, and especially the Church of Jesus Christ of Latter-Day Saints, with the writings of their founders.

[214] "Hold on" (NIV), "hold fast" (NRSV, KJV) is *katechō*, "to adhere firmly to traditions, convictions, or beliefs, hold to, hold fast" (BDAG 533, 2b).

[215] "Avoid" (NIV), "abstain from" (NRSV, KJV) is *apechomai*, which we saw in 4:3, "to avoid contact w. or use of something, keep away, abstain, refrain from" (BDAG 103, 5). "Form" (NIV, NRSV), "appearance" (KJV) is *eidos*. It has the basic meaning of "form, outward appearance." Here it means, "a variety of something, kind" (BDAG 280, 2).

May God Sanctify You and Keep You Blameless (5:23-24)

Now Paul winds down the letter with a beautiful benediction, a prayer for God's sanctifying power to immerse them completely.

> "23 May God himself, the God of peace, sanctify you through and through. May your whole spirit, soul and body be kept blameless at the coming of our Lord Jesus Christ. 24 The one who calls you is faithful and he will do it." (5:23-24)

God is identified as "the God of peace." This is Paul's fourth reference to peace in this letter. In this chapter he has encouraged them to "live in peace with each other" as a congregation (5:13). He concludes 2 Thessalonians with a similar benediction of peace from "the Lord of peace."

We've seen a theme of sanctification and holiness in this letter (2:10; 3:13), especially in regard to sexual purity (4:3-8). Here *hagiazō*, "to make holy," has the connotation, "to eliminate that which is incompatible with holiness, purify."[216] We know that God sets us apart to himself and purifies once and for all through the sacrifice of Jesus on the cross for our sins – positional holiness. But here Paul is talking about purifying our character and lifestyle – experiential holiness.

Paul prays that we might be sanctified "through and through" (NIV), "entirely" (NRSV), "wholly" (KJV). The verb is *holotelēs*, "pertaining to being totally complete, with implication of meeting a high standard, in every way complete, quite perfect."[217] So often we satisfy ourselves with a relative holiness ("I'm better than some others") or a partial holiness ("I'm better than I used to be"). But Paul calls the believers to a high, high standard of moral conduct and mental purity – "wholly sanctified"! This is a theme verse for many from the holiness tradition, such as the Nazarenes, Wesleyans, Salvation Army, and some Pentecostal groups.

Now Paul describes the extent of this holiness further. In Greek this is one long sentence.

> "May God ... sanctify you through and through. May your whole spirit, soul and body be kept blameless at the coming of our Lord Jesus Christ." (5:23)

He is saying that the holiness should not be just spiritual, or mental, or physical, but touch every part of your being! This is not partial surrender to Christ, but complete surrender to his cleansing and renewal.

Sometimes I have heard Christians get hung up on Paul's tripartite description of the totality of the person as "spirit, soul, and body" as if that is all there is. That the only

---

216 *Hagiazō*, BDAG 1, 4.
217 *Holotelēs*, BDAG 704.

proper Biblical way to describe the human being as spiritual, mental, and physical. People build whole doctrines around this phrase! The problem is that people are described in different ways in other passages of Scripture.

Psalm 16:19 – heart, soul, body

Psalm 31:9 – soul and body

Proverbs 16:24 – soul and body

Isaiah 10:18 – soul and body

Matthew 10:28 – soul and body

Hebrews 4:12 – soul and spirit, heart

Revelation 18:13 – bodies and souls

While "spirit, soul, and body" gives us insights, let's not get too dogmatic about it. This is the only place in Scripture that we are described thus.

God's Keeping Power (5:24)

Look at this verse again:

"[23] May God himself, the God of peace, sanctify you through and through. May your whole spirit, soul and body be kept blameless at the coming of our Lord Jesus Christ. [24] The one who calls you is faithful and he will do it." (1 Thessalonians 5:23-24)

Paul prays that God will *both* sanctify them *and* keep them blameless! Paul's prayer is that in total they may be "kept blameless"[218] or "preserved blameless." The verb carries the idea of "to guard," then, "to keep unharmed or undisturbed."[219]

I've met some people who are consumed with fear that they won't measure up, or be able to resist temptation. That they are too weak. That their salvation somehow rests in their own strength and efforts to live a holy life. Wrong!

Our salvation is based not on our own efforts (Ephesians 2:8-9), but on the saving death of the Son of God who died for our sins. Praise the Lord! One verse talks about the partnership we have with God in this "keeping" process:

"... Who are being protected by the power of God through faith for a salvation ready to be revealed in the last time." (1 Peter 1:5)

---

[218] "Blameless" is the adverb *amemptōs*, which we also saw in 2:10. The adjective, *amemptos*, appears in 3:13, "blameless in holiness."

[219] "Kept" (NIV, NRSV), "preserved" (KJV) is *tēreō*. The basic idea is "to guard, keep watch over." Here it has the connotation, "to cause a state, condition, or activity to continue, keep, hold, reserve, preserve someone or something," here, "keep unharmed or undisturbed" (BDAG 1002, 2b).

There's a sense in which it *is* a cooperative venture. Our faith takes hold of God's power. But don't kid yourself or beat yourself up. God's power is great enough to keep you, to preserve you blameless, so that you will stand before God's judgment on that final day, with Jesus Christ at your side, and be judged righteous. Praise God. Consider these passages that underscore God's keeping power:

> "The one who was born of God **keeps him safe**, and the evil one cannot harm him." (1 John 5:18)

> "Holy Father, **protect them** by the power of your name." (John 17:11a)

> "He will keep you strong to the end, so that you will be **blameless** on the day of our Lord Jesus Christ. God, who has called you into fellowship with his Son Jesus Christ our Lord, is faithful." (1 Corinthians 1:8-9)

> "... Christ loved the church and gave himself up for her to make her holy, cleansing her by the washing with water through the word, and to present her to himself as a radiant church, **without stain or wrinkle or any other blemish, but holy and blameless.**" (Ephesians 5:25b-27)

> "... Being confident of this, that he who began a good work in you will **carry it on to completion** until the day of Christ Jesus." (Philippians 1:6)

> "To him who is **able to keep you from falling** and to present you before his glorious presence without fault and with great joy...." (Jude 24)

Paul assures the Thessalonian church in our passage:

> "The one who calls you is faithful[220] and he will do[221] it." (5:24)

There are passages of Scripture that call us to ethical purity, and threaten us with damnation if we do not respond (for example, 1 Corinthians 6:9-11; Galatians 5:19-21). They are true; if you continue in rebellion against God you will *not* be saved! But you *do* have faith in Christ as your Savior. And this Savior is working in you to help you crucify the old nature and yield to the Spirit. You're not the person who should feel threatened. The person who continues in open and flagrant rebellion is the one who should imagine no assurance of salvation.

Ultimately, our salvation comes from God our Father through the Lord Jesus Christ. We trust in him and are saved.

---

[220] "Faithful" is *pistos*, "pertaining to being worthy of belief or trust, trustworthy, faithful, dependable, inspiring trust/faith" (BDAG 820, 1aβ).

[221] "Do" is *poieō*, "make, do," here with the idea of "to be active in some way, work, be active" (BDAG 839, 6).

"For God so loved the world that he gave his one and only Son, that whoever believes in him shall not perish but have eternal life." (John 3:16)

"The one who calls you is faithful and he will do it." (5:24)

Q5. (1 Thessalonians 5:23-24) If you met a true Christian who had no assurance of salvation, how would you explain to him or her God's power to protect and present them blameless before Christ at his coming? What is the problem of having no assurance of salvation? What is the problem of having a false assurance of salvation?
http://www.joyfulheart.com/forums/index.php?showtopic=1239

Final Words (5:25-28)

Now Paul concludes with a request for prayer and the desire that his love and affection be conveyed to all the brothers and sisters in Thessalonica.

"25 Brothers, pray for us. 26 Greet all the brothers with a holy kiss." (5:25-26)

Paul calls for prayer. The assumption behind this request is that prayer is important and effective.

"Kiss" is the noun *philēma*, a "touch with the lips, a gesture of affection or homage." It is usually devoid of erotic content in the Bible, and usually to show affection between family members. In Europe and the Middle East kissing on one or both cheeks is common. Of course, there's an erotic kiss (Song of Solomon 1:2), but Paul is distinguishing the kiss of affection and greeting from the erotic kiss by the word "holy." The "holy kiss" is found in Romans 16:16; 1 Corinthians 16:20; and 2 Corinthians 13:12, while Peter mentions the "kiss of love" (1 Peter 5:14).[222]

Now Paul commands the letter to be read.

"I charge you before the Lord to have this letter read to all the brothers." (5:27)

"Charge" (NIV, KJV), "solemnly command" (NRSV) is *horkizō*, "to give a command to someone under oath, adjure, implore."[223] Paul could be concerned that the letter may be delivered to a member of the church whose sin might be exposed in the letter. So he solemnly commands all to hear its contents read.

---

[222] Donald K. McKim, "Kiss," ISBE 3:44.
[223] *Horkizō*, BDAG 723.

Paul concludes the letter with grace – the very basis of our salvation.

"The grace of our Lord Jesus Christ be with you." (5:28)

Disciple Lessons

Paul has covered a lot of ground in this lesson, offering a number of keys to health in a congregation and in a Christian's personal life.

1. Respect for leaders (5:12-13)
2. Faithful ministry to the flock (5:14)
3. Kindness rather than vengeance (5:15)
4. Spiritual enthusiasm in joy, prayer, and thanksgiving (5:16-18)
5. Freedom of the Spirit – with discernment (19-22)
6. A desire to please Christ and live holy lives (5:23-24)
7. Prayer for Christ's mission (5:25)
8. Love and affection for one another (5:26)
9. Attention to Scripture (5:27)
10. Focus on grace (5:28)

Prayer

Father, so many of our churches are unhealthy or off-balance. I pray that you would breathe fresh air and health into our congregations so that they might be healthy, safe places to grow in Christ and focus on your mission. In Jesus' name, I pray. Amen.

Key Verses

"Make sure that nobody pays back wrong for wrong, but always try to be kind to each other and to everyone else." (1 Thessalonians 5:15)

"Be joyful always; [17] pray continually; [18] give thanks in all circumstances, for this is God's will for you in Christ Jesus." (1 Thessalonians 5:16-18)

"May God himself, the God of peace, sanctify you through and through. May your whole spirit, soul and body be kept blameless at the coming of our Lord Jesus Christ. [24] The one who calls you is faithful and he will do it." (1 Thessalonians 5:23-24)

7. Awesome Judgment at Christ's Coming (2 Thessalonians 1:1-12)

Not long after writing 1 Thessalonians, Paul and his missionary band, which included Silas and Timothy, wrote a second letter from Corinth. It is a stronger letter, no doubt prompted by some report of renewed problems in the church. The letter centers around two problems that were present when 1 Thessalonians was written but haven't been corrected: a misunderstanding about Christ's return and a continued problem with idle believers who persist in being dependent upon the church, rather than finding gainful employment. Near the beginning of this second letter, Paul also encourages the Thessalonians to stand fast in spite of the persecution they are experiencing, and explains the severe judgment that their persecutors face.

Salutation (1:1-2)

The letter's salutation is similar to that found in the first letter.

> "[1] Paul, Silas and Timothy, To the church of the Thessalonians in God our Father and the Lord Jesus Christ: [2] Grace and peace to you from God the Father and the Lord Jesus Christ." (1:1-2)

Though the letter is penned in the name of Paul, Silas, and Timothy, it's quite likely that Paul was the chief author.

Growing in Faith, Love, and Perseverance (1:3-5)

Paul begins with the traditional introductory thanksgiving or blessing that appears in correspondence of that time.

> "[3] We ought always to thank God for you, brothers, and rightly[224] so, because your faith is growing more and more, and the love every one of you has for each other is increasing. [4] Therefore, among God's churches we boast about your perseverance and faith in all the persecutions and trials you are enduring. [5] All this is evidence that God's judgment is right, and as a result you will be counted worthy of the kingdom of God, for which you are suffering." (1:3-5)

---

[224] "Right/ly" (NIV, NRSV), "meet" (KJV) is *axios*, "befitting, congruous, corresponding," to a thing (BDAG 52, bα).

Paul doesn't begin with chiding, but with praise. He thanks God for two things:

1.   Growing[225] faith.

2.   Increasing[226] love for one another.

This would be expected in a healthy church, but it is remarkable in light of their circumstances. This young church is undergoing significant persecution and trials – and in spite of that they are growing in Christian character. Praise the Lord! Paul uses three words to describe the stresses that they are facing:

1. Persecution (1:4). The word is *diōgmos*, "a program or process designed to harass and oppress someone, persecution."[227] Christians face occasional slights or put-downs from the non-believers. This is uncomfortable – and sometimes is enough to silence us (to our shame). But this is hardly persecution. What the Thessalonians were facing was an organized program to make their life miserable. It was apparently begun by the Jewish community in Thessalonica, and then continued by the secular authorities.

Sometimes, persecution can decimate a congregation or Christian movement in a region. However, persecution can have some positive effects as well. In Thessalonica, no doubt, it spared the church from hangers-on who weren't really believers, since being a Christian was costly. Church Father Tertullian observed in 197 AD, "The blood of the martyrs is the seed of the Church."[228] Rather than destroying the church, persecution – even severe persecution – ultimately purifies the church and can ultimately cause it to grow. Persecution is a stressor that can strengthen your spiritual life if you let it.

2. Trials or tribulations (1:4). "Trials" (NIV), "afflictions" (NRSV), "tribulations" (KJV) translate the noun *thlipsis*, literally, "pressing, pressure." Here it is used in a metaphorical sense, "trouble that inflicts distress, oppression, affliction, tribulation."[229] The word is used to describe the "great tribulation" at the end of the age (Matthew 24:21; Revelation 7:14), but can also refer to problems of any sort. It can describe all kinds of difficulties that face us in life – family problems, financial pressures, job concerns, health problems, etc.

When a young tree is planted in its final location, it is often supported by a couple of wood stakes to keep the tree from blowing over during a windstorm. But if improperly

---

[225] "Growing more and more" (NIV), "growing abundantly" (NRSV), "groweth exceedingly" (KJV) is *hyperauxanō*, "grow wonderfully, increase abundantly" (BDAG 1032).

[226] "Increasing" (NIV, NRSV), "aboundeth" (KJV) is *pleonazō*, "to become more and more, so as to be in abundance, be/become more or be/become great, be present in abundance, grow, increase" (BDAG 824, 1).

[227] *Diōgmos*, BDAG 253.

[228] Tertullian, *Apologeticus*, 30.

[229] *Thlipsis*, BDAG 457, 1.

applied, these stakes can harm the long-term health of the tree. The tie fastening the tree to the stakes can be so tight that the tree doesn't move in the wind. If the new tree doesn't move, it doesn't develop the strong fibers that it will need as it matures. The tie to the support needs to be loose enough that the trunk has room to move back and forth in the wind. Trees – and humans – can grow strong through stress. If you've ever seen a tree in a high-wind, you may marvel at the strength of the trunk that has grown strong in spite of – indeed, because of – its harsh environment.

It is no accident that after his baptism, the Father purposely led Jesus into a situation of intense stress:

> "At once the Spirit sent him out into the desert, and he was in the desert forty days, being tempted by Satan. He was with the wild animals, and angels attended him." (Mark 1:12-13)

At no time did Jesus cease being the eternal Son of God. But when he became human, he had emptied himself of some of his divine prerogatives (Philippians 2:7). He was pure, he was holy, but he was untested. In order to destroy the works of the devil in his ministry (1 John 3:8), Jesus needed to meet Satan and overcome him at the beginning of his ministry. Rather than being drained by the encounter, Jesus emerged from the desert strengthened "in the power of the Spirit" (Luke 4:14).

3. Suffering (1:5b). Next, Paul speaks of "the kingdom of God, for which you are suffering."[230] The verb *paschō* is used of Jesus' suffering at the hands of his tormentors and on the cross, where it means "to suffer death" itself. The related noun is *pathos*, from which we get our English word "pathos," "evoking pity or compassion," and prefix *patho-*, which combined with other words, denotes disease and suffering, such as "pathology," "pathogen," etc.

The trials and struggles we experience are by no means trivial. They entail real suffering. But the Thessalonians had experienced what many Christians have discovered over the ages, that we grow more when our faith is tested than when all is going well. In fact, trials of our faith are an intentional part of God's growth plan for his children.

The Wonderful Fruits of Testing (1:3-5)

If the experience of suffering trials and persecutions is intense, the fruit thereof is sweet.

---

[230] "Suffering/suffer" is *paschō*, "experience something," but mostly in the New Testament in an unfavorable sense, "suffer, endure" (BDAG 785, 3aβ).

"[3b] Your **faith** is growing more and more, and the **love** every one of you has for each other is increasing. [4] Therefore, among God's churches we boast about your **perseverance** and faith in all the persecutions and trials you are **enduring**. All this is evidence that God's judgment is right, and as a result you will be **counted worthy** of the kingdom of God, for which you are suffering." (1:3-5)

Paul points out four important results of our struggles:

1. **Growing faith**. When we see God faithful to answer our fervent prayers in the midst of our trials, our faith blossoms. If God can help us in this situation, we reason, he can help us in any situation. "If God is for us, who can be against us?" (Romans 8:31). Strong faith comes from experiencing God's faithfulness in the crucible of life.

2. **Increasing love**. People who go through difficulties together find that the bonds that unite them become stronger and stronger. The Thessalonians are loving each other more and more *because of* their common persecutions and tribulations.

3. **Perseverance**. "Perseverance" (NIV), "steadfastness" (NRSV), "patience" (KJV) is *hypomonē*, "the capacity to hold out or bear up in the face of difficulty, patience, endurance, fortitude, steadfastness, perseverance."[231] When Christians come out on the other side of troubles, having endured the worst Satan could throw at them, they are stronger. They know they can outlast troubles in the future without giving in. Jesus is stronger than our trials.

4. **Counted worthy**.[232] Of course, in the ultimate sense, we deserve nothing. We are products of God's grace, pure and simple. But in the sense Paul mentions here, the Thessalonians' emergence from trials and persecutions with stronger faith, love, and perseverance is a sign that they have stood the test and are worthy of the kingdom to which they have been called. Were they perfect? No. But, over all, the fruit of the Spirit could be seen in their lives.

Q1. (2 Thessalonians 1:3-5) In what ways do persecution, pressure, and stress help us grow strong in Christ? What would we be like without the testing of our faith?
http://www.joyfulheart.com/forums/index.php?showtopic=1240

---

[231] *Hypomonē*, BDAG 1039, 1. At the end of verse 5, the verb "enduring/endure," *anechō*, "to undergo something onerous or troublesome without giving in, endure" (BDAG 78, 2).

[232] "Counted worthy" (NIV, KJV), "make you worthy" (NRSV) is *kataxioō*, "to consider someone worthy to receive some privilege, benefit, or recognition; consider worthy" (BDAG 523). Similar in meaning to *axioō* in verse 11, "to consider suitable for requital or for receipt of something, consider worthy, deserving" (BDAG 94, 1).

Counted Worthy of the Kingdom (1:5)

Paul's main theme for this letter is eschatology, the Coming of Christ – and the Antichrist – in the last days. The next section is about God's just judgment when Christ returns and serves as a transition to Paul's main theme.

> "[5] All this is evidence that God's judgment is right, and as a result you will be counted worthy of the kingdom of God, for which you are suffering." (1:5)

Verse 5 is difficult. Something is evidence or a "plain indication"[233] that God's judgment is right, but what is it?

On the surface, at least, it's hard to see how persecution and affliction would be evidence of God's righteous judgment.[234] As a result, most commentators see the evidence as the believers' endurance and faith *in the face* of persecution as the sign, and point to a similar usage in Philippians 1:28.

> "... I will know that you stand firm in one spirit, contending as one man for the faith of the gospel without being frightened in any way by those who oppose you. This is a **sign**[235] to them that they will be destroyed, but that you will be saved – and that by God." (Philippians 1:27-28)

Doubtless, the Thessalonian believers could not have exhibited such a remarkable attitude of endurance and faith unless God had worked it in them.

Now Paul lays out several important principles about judgment:

God is Just (1:6a)

Paul begins to describe the nature of God's justice.

> "[6] God is just: He will pay back trouble to those who trouble you [7] and give relief to you who are troubled, and to us as well." (1:6-7a)

First, Paul explains that God is "just" (NIV, NRSV), that his judgment is a "righteous thing" (KJV). The adjective is *dikaios*. The neuter here denotes that which is "obligatory

---

[233] "Evidence" (NIV, NRSV), "manifest token" (KJV) is *endeigma*, "the proof of something, evidence, plain indication" (BDAG 332).

[234] Wanamaker (pp. 220-221), in a rather complex argument, cites Jouette M. Bassler ("The Enigmatic Sign: 2 Thessalonians 1:5," *Catholic Biblical Quarterly* 46 (1984), pp. 501-506) to the effect that verse 5 represents an emerging theology of suffering. The believers assumed that the day of the Lord had already come (2:1-12), but their continued persecution didn't fit with this, causing questions about the justice of God. Wanamaker holds that the verse indicates that God's justice is shown in that persecution is making them worthy of the kingdom. The problem with this view is that *kataxioō*, means "to count worthy" or "to declare worthy," not "to make worthy" (Stott, *Message*, p. 146, citing Lightfoot, *Notes on the Epistles of Paul* (1895), p. 105 and Morris, *Thessalonians*, p. 116.

[235] *Endeixis*, "something that points to or serves as an indicator of something, sign, omen" (BDAG 332, 1).

in view of certain requirements of justice, right, fair, equitable."[236] God gave the Mosaic law that laid down righteous principles by which God's people were to live. God *defines* what righteousness is. This theme is seen often in the Old Testament.

"Will not the Judge of all the earth **do right**?" (Genesis 18:25)

"He is the Rock, his works are **perfect**,
and all his ways are **just**.
A faithful God who does **no wrong,**
upright and just is he." (Deuteronomy 32:4)

"The LORD is **righteous, he loves justice**;
upright men will see his face." (Psalm 11:7)

"The LORD ... comes to judge the earth.
He will judge the world in righteousness
and the peoples with **equity**." (Psalm 98:9)

God Exacts Just Retribution (1:6b-7a)

"[6] God is just: He will pay back trouble to those who trouble you [7] and give relief to you who are troubled, and to us as well." (1:6-7a)

In our culture, some believe that the highest goal of prisons is rehabilitation, not retribution, that somehow retribution is an inferior motive. But here the purpose of God's justice on the Day of the Lord is retribution. In 1:6b we find a word variously translated, "pay back" (NIV), "repay" (NRSV), "recompense" (KJV). The word is *antapodidōmi*, "to exact retribution, repay, pay back."[237]

God pays back trouble (*thlipsis*) to those who trouble or afflict (*thlibō*) you. He pays back in kind. This is the ancient principle of proportional retribution. Indeed, the idea of just consequences or recompense for actions is at the basis of rudimentary parental discipline as well as civil law. Our English word "vengeance" means, "punishment inflicted in retaliation for an injury or offense, retribution."[238] Only the idea of "with a vengeance" suggests excessive retribution. "Revenge" refers to a personal rather than judicial response, "to avenge (as oneself) usually by retaliating in kind or degree."

---

[236] *Dikaios*, BDAG 242, 2.

[237] *Antapodidōmi*, BDAG 87, 2. This is a compound verb formed from *anti-* "for something received, in return" + *apodidōmi*, "to deliver," specifically, "to requite, recompense." In English, "recompense" means "to give something to by way of compensation (as for a service rendered or damage incurred), to return in kind." "Retribution" is "recompense, reward."

[238] *Merriam-Webster's 11th Collegiate Dictionary.*

Because of the fallen nature of mankind, the Mosaic Covenant limits the amount of personal retribution that can be exacted by an individual – no more than the injury.

> "If there is serious injury, you are to take life for life, eye for eye, tooth for tooth, hand for hand, foot for foot, burn for burn, wound for wound, bruise for bruise." (Exodus 21:23-25)

When Jesus came, he revealed that the basic concept of the Torah is love – love for God and love for your neighbor. Sometimes, people contend that love makes justice obsolete. Jesus doesn't teach this. Jesus speaks of just judgment. Indeed, judgment is a major theme in Jesus' ministry; the words "judge" and "judgment" appear 55 times in the Gospels.

We Are to Leave Vengeance to God

Though God brings righteous vengeance against the wicked – and governmental authorities are charged with executing just punishment on earth (Romans 13:4) – we Christians are to refrain from vengeance in our own personal lives, as we saw in 1 Thessalonians 1:15 (Lesson 6; also Romans 12:17-19). Vengeance is reserved to God.

God is able to balance love and justice, though we find it very difficult in practice. Notice how God combines mercy and justice in these verses:

> "The LORD, the LORD, the compassionate and gracious God, slow to anger, abounding in love and faithfulness, maintaining love to thousands, and forgiving wickedness, rebellion and sin. Yet he does not leave the guilty unpunished; he punishes the children and their children for the sin of the fathers to the third and fourth generation." (Exodus 34:6-7)

> "Love and faithfulness meet together;
> righteousness and peace kiss each other." (Psalm 85:10)

> "Mercy triumphs over judgment!" (James 2:13b)

Q2. (2 Thessalonians 1:6-7) Would God be just if he did *not* punish sin? What is the difference between rehabilitation and retribution? When does a Christian's rehabilitation take place? When does a sinner's retribution take place? How do you balance love and justice?

http://www.joyfulheart.com/forums/index.php?showtopic=1241

When Christ Returns He Will Bring Terrible Judgment (1:7b-10)

We can trust the God of love to judge justly, even though that's difficult for us. When Christ returns, those who have resisted and rebelled against him will receive terrible judgment!

> "7b This will happen when the Lord Jesus is revealed
> from heaven in blazing fire with his powerful angels." (1:7b)

When Christ is finally revealed in his Second Coming, all secrets will be revealed too.[239] He comes with "blazing fire,"[240] which jives with other verses about the Lord's coming (Isaiah 66:15-16; 2 Peter 3:10). Fire and judgment are often joined in the Bible.

The terrible judgment of God is given on the Day of the Lord.

> "8 He will punish those who do not know God and do not obey the gospel of our Lord Jesus. 9 They will be punished with everlasting destruction and shut out from the presence of the Lord and from the majesty of his power 10 on the day he comes to be glorified in his holy people and to be marveled at among all those who have believed. This includes you, because you believed our testimony to you." (1:8-10)

Let's look at the passage piece by piece to see exactly what it says. The text itself is not difficult. But two theological issues it raises are – the existence of hell and the question of "what about the heathen?" – which we examine briefly in Appendices 1 and 2.

Punishment upon Those Who Reject and Disobey (1:8)

First, though, let's look at the text.

> "He will punish those who do not know God and do not obey the gospel of our Lord Jesus." (1:8)

The objects of punishment are people who do not know God and/or do not obey the gospel. We can understand why people should be punished for not obeying[241] God when they know better. But what about those who have never heard? Can people be blamed for not "knowing"[242] God, if they've never heard? This is a difficult question. I

---

[239] The verb "revealed" is literally, "in the revelation." It uses a preposition "in" plus the noun *apokalypsis*. The basic idea is "uncovering," here used figuratively, "making fully known, revelation, disclosure"(BDAG 112, 1c). It refers to the coming of Jesus at the *parousia*, when all secrets are revealed.

[240] "Blazing fire" (NIV), "flaming fire" (NRSV, KJV) is two nouns –*pyr*, "fire" (from which we get our word "pyre) and *phlox*, "flame."

[241] Obey" is *hypakouō*, "to follow instructions, obey, follow, be subject to," (BDAG 1029, 1). from Homer down; "to listen, hearken," here, ""to hearken to a command," *i.e.* "to obey, be obedient unto, submit to," (so in Greek writings from Herodotus down) (Thayer 638, 2).

[242] "Know" is *oida*. Here it is more than, "have information about." It has the sense, "be intimately acquainted with or stand in a close relation to, know." To know God, that is, not only to know theoretical-

explore that a bit in Appendix 1, "Can Heathen Who Have Never Heard the Gospel Be Saved?" In brief, Paul is not talking here about earnest seekers among the heathen, but judgment upon those who rebel against the light they have received and act contrary to the sense of right and wrong God has put within their consciences.

Everlasting, Conscious Punishment (1:9)

The noun "punish"[243] in verse 8 and the noun "punishment"[244] in verse 9 both involve the idea of retribution, paying back to people what they deserve. We talked about this already in 1:6 above.

Wayne Grudem defines "hell" as "a place of eternal conscious[245] punishment for the wicked."[246] That definition seems to be well supported by our passage. Let's look at the elements of this punishment in verse 9.

> "They will be punished with everlasting destruction and shut out from the presence of the Lord and from the majesty of his power." (1:9)

1. Everlasting.[247]   Punishment is unending, it lasts forever. In the same way that eternal life is forever, so is everlasting punishment. Some people object that this isn't fair, it is disproportionate, that sin committed in time doesn't merit punishment for a thousand lifetimes, eternal punishment. But to rebel against the infinite God is an infinite crime. To reject his love in sending his own Son who died for our sins is to turn down your only chance at forgiveness. If you expect to confront the Judge of All the Earth with being unfair in his punishment, good luck.

---

ly of God's existence, but to have a positive relationship with God, or not to know God, that is, wanting to know nothing about God (BDAG 693, 2). He probably has the Gentiles in mind (1 Thessalonians 4:5; Galatians 4:8-9; Romans 1:28; Ephesians 2:12; 1 Corinthians 1:21; 1 John 4:7-8; John 8:19, 55; 15:21; 16:3; 17:3).

[243] "Punish" (NIV), "inflicting vengeance" (NRSV), "taking vengeance" (KJV) is two words, *didōmi*, "give" and *ekdikēsis*, "penalty inflicted on wrongdoers," absolutely, "punishment" (BDAG 302, 3). It is from the verb *endikeō*, "to inflict appropriate penalty for wrong done" (of special significance in an honor/shame-oriented society) "punish, take vengeance for something" (BDAG 300, 2).

[244] "Punish/punishment" is two words, the verb *tinō*, "pay" and the noun *dikē*, "punishment meted out as legal penalty, punishment, penalty." Together, the phrase means, "pay a penalty, suffer punishment, be punished of or with something" (BDAG 256, 1).

[245] The "conscious" part of the definition is amply supported by Luke 16:23-24 and Revelation 14:10-11.

[246] Wayne Grudem, *Systematic Theology: An Introduction to Biblical Doctrine* (Zondervan, 1994, 2000), pp. 1148-1153.

[247] "Everlasting" (NIV, KJV), "eternal" (NRSV) is the adjective *aiōnios*, here, "pertaining to a period of unending duration, without end" (BDAG 33, 3).

2. Destruction. "Destruction" is *olethros*, "a state of destruction, ruin, death."[248] It *can* infer annihilation, but does not have to. Rather it refers to the harmful and destructive effects of final judgment on unbelievers. Some people (including Jehovah's Witness and Seventh Day Adventists) can't see how God's love is compatible with conscious eternal punishment. So they conclude that the "destruction" *must* mean annihilation, that is, punishment for a time ending in complete termination of existence.[249] That sounds good, perhaps, but annihilation doesn't fit with what the Bible actually teaches – a state of complete ruin that lasts forever. Consider these passages:

> *Daniel's prophecy*: "At that time your people – everyone whose name is found written in the book – will be delivered. Multitudes who sleep in the dust of the earth will awake: some to everlasting life, **others to shame and everlasting contempt**. Those who are wise will shine like the brightness of the heavens, and those who lead many to righteousness, like the stars for ever and ever." (Daniel 12:2-3)

> *John the Baptist*: "His winnowing fork is in his hand, and he will clear his threshing floor, gathering his wheat into the barn and **burning up the chaff with unquenchable fire.**" (Matthew 3:12; Luke 3:17)

> *Jesus:* "Do not be afraid of those who kill the body but cannot kill the soul. Rather, be afraid of the One who can **destroy both soul and body in hell.**" (Matthew 10:28)

> *Jesus:* "It is better for you to enter life maimed or crippled than to have two hands or two feet and be **thrown into eternal fire**." (Matthew 18:8)

> *Jesus:* "Then he will say to those on his left, 'Depart from me, you who are cursed, **into the eternal fire prepared for the devil and his angels.**'" (Matthew 25:41)

> *Jesus*: "Then they will go away to **eternal punishment**, but the righteous to **eternal life**." (Matthew 25:46)

> *Writer of Hebrews*: "The elementary teachings (of) ... **eternal judgment**." (Hebrews 6:2)

> *Jude*: The punishment of Sodom and Gomorrah serves as "an example of those who suffer **the punishment of eternal fire**." (Jude 7)

> *Revelation*: "If anyone worships the beast and his image ... he will be tormented with burning sulfur in the presence of the holy angels and of the Lamb. And **the smoke of their torment rises for ever and ever. There is no rest day or night**...." (Revelation 14:9-11)

> *Revelation*: "He has condemned the great prostitute who corrupted the earth by her adulteries.... The **smoke from her goes up for ever and ever.**" (Revelation 19:1, 3)

---

[248] *Olethros*, BDAG 702, 1.

[249] Most recently annihilationism has been argued by Rob Bell, *Love Wins: A Book About Heaven, Hell, and the Fate of Every Person Who Ever Lived* (HarperOne, 2011).

Revelation: And the devil, who deceived them, was thrown into the lake of burning sulfur, where the beast and the false prophet had been thrown. **They will be tormented day and night for ever and ever**.... If anyone's name was not found written in the book of life, he was thrown into the lake of fire." (Revelation 20:10, 15)

In light of these passages, it's very difficult for me to believe in annihilation rather than everlasting punishment. You don't have to like it. You don't have to take pleasure it in – God doesn't (Ezekiel 33:11). But it's pretty clear that the Bible teaches everlasting conscious punishment.

3. Shut out forever from Christ's presence.

"They will be punished with everlasting destruction and shut out from[250] the presence[251] of the Lord and from the majesty of his power." (1:9)

Those who don't know Jesus personally have little understanding of what a blessing his presence is. They see Christianity as a religion in which you relate to God through various rituals. So the idea of "the presence of the Lord" has little meaning. Secular people see heaven (if they believe in it) as a place of rest and goodness and reunion with friends. But the essence of heaven from a Biblical point of view is being with Jesus. Paul would "prefer to be away from the body and at home[252] (KJV "present") with the Lord" (2 Corinthians 5:8). He says, "I desire to depart and be with Christ, which is better by far" (Philippians 1:23b). For the Christian, the ultimate that we look forward to is expressed in, "they shall see his face" (Revelation 22:4). Now imagine being deprived forever of being with Christ – much less being deprived of all your believing relatives who are with Christ.

Recently I conducted a funeral for an aged member of our church who had moved into a distant convalescent hospital a few years before. Her wayward son told me that his mother had said, "If you aren't in heaven, I don't want to be there. I want to be where you are." Now, I can understand a mother's intense love for her son. But it's tragic that she loves her children more than she loves Jesus Christ, for Jesus himself said,

"Anyone who loves his son or daughter more than me is not worthy of me." (Matthew 10:37)

Who is your first love? Is Jesus the center of your hope for heaven?

4. Shut out from Christ's glory.

---

[250] "Shut out from" (NIV), "separated from" (NRSV), "from" (KJV) is the preposition *apo*, "to indicate distance from a point, away from" (BDAG 106, 4).

[251] "Presence" is *prosōpon*, literally, "face," here in the figurative sense of "personal presence or relational circumstance" (BDAG 887, 1bβ Aleph).

[252] *Endēmeō*, "to be in a familiar place, to be at home"(BDAG 332).

"They will be punished with everlasting destruction and shut out from the presence of the Lord and from the **majesty of his power**." (1:9)

"Majesty" (NIV), "glory" (NRSV, KJV) is *doxa*, "the condition of being bright or shining, brightness, splendor, radiance (a distinctive aspect of Hebrew *kabod*)."[253] That may not mean much to you until you read the prophecies in Isaiah and Revelation:

> "Go into the rocks,
> **hide in the ground from** dread of the LORD
> and the **splendor**[254] **of his majesty**!" (Isaiah 2:10, 19, 21).

> "Then the kings of the earth, the princes, the generals, the rich, the mighty, and every slave and every free man hid in caves and among the rocks of the mountains. They called to the mountains and the rocks, 'Fall on us and **hide us from the face of him** who sits on the throne and from the wrath of the Lamb! For the great day of their wrath has come, and **who can stand?**'" (Revelation 6:15-17)

When Christ comes, he will come with a light and glory of such intensity than sinners cannot look upon him or stand before him. It will be like trying to look directly into a huge, blinding arc-light.

> "The Son of Man is to come with his angels **in the glory of his Father**, and then he will repay everyone for what has been done." (Matthew 16:27)

> "Then the sign of the Son of Man will appear in heaven, and then all the tribes of the earth will mourn, and they will see 'the Son of Man coming on the clouds of heaven' with power and **great glory**." (Matthew 24:30)

When the Father sits on his judgment throne, everyone will flee from his presence because of his awesome glory.

> "Then I saw a great white throne and the one who sat on it; the earth and the heaven **fled from his presence**, and no place was found for them." (Revelation 20:11)

Verse 9 in our passage is truly an awesome and frightening verse. If it is true, then we would be fools not to flee to the mercy found in Jesus. If you believe it is false, then you'll keep on living like you want. The most famous verse in the Bible introduces this awesome truth, but in a positive way.

> "For God so loved the world that he gave his one and only Son, that whoever believes in him **shall not perish**[255] but have eternal life." (John 3:16)

---

[253] *Doxa*, BDAG 257, 1 or 2. The lexicographer suggests that *doxa* here may mean, "a state of being magnificent, greatness, splendor."

[254] "Splendor" (NIV), "glory" (KJV) is *hādār*, "splendor, honor," which is used synonymously with *kabod*, "glory," in a number of places (TWOT #477b).

Q3. (2 Thessalonians 1:9) According to verse 9, what kind of punishment will unbelievers experience? One definition of "hell" is "a place of eternal conscious punishment for the wicked." What parts of this definition are confirmed in verse 9. Which parts of the definition trouble you? Why?

http://www.joyfulheart.com/forums/index.php?showtopic=1242

Q4. (2 Thessalonians 1:9) How might you describe Christ's glory? How will his glory be terrifying to unbelievers? If heaven involves sharing this glory forever, what would it be like to be excluded forever from the glory? In what ways is the phrase "outer darkness" a helpful description of hell?

http://www.joyfulheart.com/forums/index.php?showtopic=1243

Christ Is to Be Glorified (1:10)

The final part of this passage tells when this judgment will take place:

> "... On the day he comes to be glorified in his holy people and to be marveled at among all those who have believed. This includes you, because you believed our testimony to you." (1:10)

There will come a time when Christ will be glorified[256] in the midst[257] of his saints, his holy people. A time when we will look at him with amazement and wonder.[258] The Apostle John looks forward to this day:

---

[255] "Perish" is *apollymi*, "perish, be ruined, die," especially of eternal death (Luke 19:10; John 10:28; 17:12; Romans 2:12; 1 Corinthians 1:18; 2 Corinthians 2:15; 4:3; 2 Thessalonians 2:10; etc.).

[256] "Glorified" is *endoxazomai*, "to be held in high esteem, be glorified, honored" (1:10, 12). Thayer: that his glory may be seen in the saints, that is, in the glory, blessedness, conferred on them" (Thayer, 214).

[257] The preposition is *en*, "in" which could be translated as "by" (NRSV), or "in, among" (NIV, KJV).

[258] "Marveled at" (NIV, NRSV), "admired" (KJV) is *thaumazō*, "to be extraordinarily impressed or disturbed by something," here trans. "admire, wonder at, respect (persons)" (BDAG 445, 1bβ).

> "Dear friends, now we are children of God, and what we will be has not yet been made known. But we know that when he appears, we shall be like him, for we shall see him as he is." (1 John 3:2)

What a Day that will be!

Raising the Hard Questions

Now we need to examine a couple of theological questions that are difficult to answer. These are questions that our non-Christian friends raise before us as their excuses not to believe. These are not questions of "What does the Bible teach?" They are rather questions of, "I don't like what the Bible teaches, so how can it be true logically?" These are the types of questions answered by Christian apologetics. To treat these in greater detail, I've include an outline of the issue in two appendices:

- Appendix 1. Can Heathen Who Have Never Heard the Gospel Be Saved?
- Appendix 2. How Can There Be a Hell Like the Bible Describes?

I encourage you to read both of these appendices.

Fulfilling Every Good Purpose (1:11-12)

Paul concludes this section on God's severe judgment on the Thessalonians' persecutors, with a softer tone toward the Thessalonians themselves.

> "[11] With this in mind, we constantly pray for you, that our God may count you worthy of his calling, and that by his power he may fulfill[259] every good purpose of yours and every act prompted by your faith. [12] We pray this so that the name of our Lord Jesus may be glorified in you, and you in him, according to the grace of our God and the Lord Jesus Christ." (1:11-12)

It is a three-fold prayer, that God will

1. Count you worthy of his calling (see on 1:5),
2. Fulfill your good intentions and faith-filled actions, and
3. Glorify Christ in you.

All of this is predicated on the "grace of our God and the Lord Jesus Christ" (1:12b). As we've seen, mankind's only hope is God's grace, his unmerited favor towards us. How can we understand love that gives, and gives, and gives again at the greatest cost, that we might find salvation and eternal life? Though we can't fully understand such love, we rejoice in it and celebrate our great Savior!

---

[259] "Fulfill" is *plēroō*, "to bring to completion that which was already begun, complete, finish" (BDAG 828, 3).

Prayer

Father, such terrible judgment frightens us and is abhorrent to us. It's hard for us to understand. But then, such gracious love is hard for us to understand as well. Thank you for your redemption. Help us to be faithful to proclaim your love in a dark world before it is too late for them. Help us, through the Holy Spirit, to save a brand from the burning,[260] to help "turn a sinner from the error of his way ... to save him from death and cover over a multitude of sins."[261] In Jesus' holy name, we pray. Amen.

Key Verses

"God is just: He will pay back trouble to those who trouble you and give relief to you who are troubled, and to us as well. This will happen when the Lord Jesus is revealed from heaven in blazing fire with his powerful angels. He will punish those who do not know God and do not obey the gospel of our Lord Jesus. They will be punished with everlasting destruction and shut out from the presence of the Lord and from the majesty of his power. (2 Thessalonians 1:6-9)

[260] Zechariah 3:2.

[261] James 5:20.

8. The Coming Antichrist (2 Thessalonians 2:1-3:5)

The first chapter of 2 Thessalonians dealt primarily with preliminary greetings and encouragement in the face of persecution, though it included a pretty heavy section about the judgment of the wicked. Now Paul gets to the first of his two major themes:

1. The coming of the Antichrist (2:1-3:5, Lesson 8), and

2. A strong exhortation to idlers not to be dependent upon others (3:6-18, Lesson 9).

The Day of the Lord (2:1-2)

In 1 Thessalonians 4:13-5:11 (Lesson 5), Paul had comforted the church concerning Christ's coming as it related to their members who had already died. But now the congregation seems upset about another issue related to Christ's coming.

> "[1] Concerning the coming of our Lord Jesus Christ and our being gathered to him, we ask you, brothers, [2] not to become easily unsettled or alarmed by some prophecy, report or letter supposed to have come from us,[262] saying that the day of the Lord has already come." (2:1-2)

Apparently someone has brought them a message – purportedly from Paul – to the effect that Christ had already come, and that somehow they must have missed the rapture! It's amazing how false rumors can take on a life of their own.

So Paul patiently explains that the Antichrist must come first. Christ will come only after the appearance of the Antichrist. Without this chapter (and some information in Revelation 13), we wouldn't know much about the Antichrist, so I guess it's good for us that Paul had to give the Thessalonian church this explanation.

Paul begins with three terms that we've already met in our study.

- **"Coming"** is *parousia*, "coming, advent." This word became the official term for a visit of a person of high rank, especially of kings and emperors visiting a province."[263] The term occurs several times in these two letters (1 Thessalonians 2:19; 3:13; 4:15; and 2 Thessalonians 2:1, 8).

---

[262] "Supposed to have to come from us" (NIV) uses the particle *hōs*, "as, like," here, "marker introducing the perspective from which a person, thing, or activity is viewed or understood as to character, function, or role, as," in our verse with focus on what is objectively false or erroneous, "alleged to be from us" (BDAG 1103, 3c).

[263] *Parousia*, BDAG 780, 2bα.

- **Gathered**.[264] The gathering of God's people is popularly known as the rapture. We discussed that at some length at 1 Thessalonians 4:17 (Lesson 5).
- **Day of the Lord**. The "day of the Lord" (which we saw in 1 Thessalonians 5:2) refers to the day that Jesus will return. It has both a positive and negative connotation. For those who are under God's wrath, it will be a terrible day of judgment, but for those awaiting Christ's return it will be a day of joy, triumph, and reward. The phrase "day of the Lord" is used many times in the Old Testament prophets with reference to the day when God will come with judgment upon sin and sinners.[265] We also see the phrase in the New Testament.[266]

The reason that Paul must write the congregation is because they are upset and confused about eschatology, the study of the Last Days. Look at the words Paul uses to describe their state:

- **"Unsettled"** (NIV), **"shaken"** (NRSV, KJV) is *saleuō*, "to disturb inwardly, disturb, shake."[267]

- **"Alarmed"** (NIV) is *throeō*, "cry out, tell out, speak, announce," here in the sense "be inwardly aroused, be disturbed or frightened."[268]

What makes it particular disturbing is that someone has spread this false teaching that Christ has already come in a letter claiming to be from Paul. Paul dashes off this letter to set the record straight. You'll notice at the end of the epistle (3:17), he points to a final note in his own handwriting as an indication that this letter is authentic.

Now Paul explains the order of events surrounding Christ's coming.

> "Don't let anyone deceive you in any way, for that day will not come until the rebellion occurs and the **man of lawlessness** is revealed, the man doomed to destruction." (2:3)

---

[264] "Being gathered/gathering together" is *episynagōgē*, "meeting," here refers to "the action of assembling" (BDAG 382, 2).

[265] The phrase "day of the Lord" is found in these Old Testament passages: Isaiah 13:6, 9; Jeremiah 46:10; Lamentations 2:22; Ezekiel 7:19; 13:5; 30:3; Joel 1:15; 2:1, 11, 31; 3:14; Amos 5:18, 20; Obadiah 15; Zephaniah 1:7-8, 14, 18; 2:2; Zechariah 14:1; and Malachi 4:5.

[266] The phrase "day of the Lord" appears in the New Testament at Acts 2:20; 1 Corinthians 5:5; 2 Corinthians 1:14; 1 Thessalonians 5:2; here, and in 2 Peter 3:10.

[267] *Saleuō*, BDAG 912, 2.

[268] *Throeō*, BDAG 460.

Q1. (1 Thessalonians 2:1-3) In what way were the Thessalonians confused? What is the order of Christ's coming in relation to the revealing of the Antichrist?
http://www.joyfulheart.com/forums/index.php?showtopic=1244

The "Man of Lawlessness" or Antichrist in the Bible

While Paul uses the term "man of lawlessness" to describe the evil figure that will be revealed in the last days, the generic term for this figure is the Antichrist.

The actual term "antichrist" occurs only in John's letters. "Antichrist" (a transliteration from the Greek word *antichristos*) means, literally, "adversary of the Messiah."[269]

However, in the apocalyptic literature of the Bible we see various mentions of this figure who will appear in the end times as an opponent of God and his Messiah.

- **Daniel** seems to refer to this antichrist figure as "the ruler who will come," who will set up in the temple of God "an abomination that causes desolation" (Daniel 9:26-27).
- **Jesus** warns, "So when you see standing in the holy place 'the abomination that causes desolation,' spoken of through the prophet Daniel," you are to flee (Matthew 24:15).
- **Paul**, in our passage, seems to be referring to this same antichrist figure as "the man of lawlessness," who will set himself up in God's temple, proclaiming himself to be God (2:3-4). Paul insists that this figure has not yet appeared on the world scene (2:7).
- **John.** The Apostle John, writing about 90 AD, notes that while the Antichrist himself had not yet come, his spirit is already in the world in the form of many antichrists (1 John 2:18, 22; 4:3; 2 John 7).
- **Revelation** refers to the antichrist figure as the "beast coming out of the sea" (Revelation 13:1), who acts as a puppet of Satan (13: 4), makes war against Christian believers (13:7), and causes the unbelievers to worship him (13:8), aided by the "false prophet," the "beast out of the earth" (Revelation 13:11-18).

---

[269] *Antichristos*, BDAG 91; The Greek word *"antichristos"* is made up of two words: the prefix *anti-*, "acting in the place of" and "opposed to" + *christos*, "Christ." See also Duane F. Watson, "Antichrist," DLNT 50-53.

This figure may also be mentioned by other prophecies – we're not trying to be exhaustive here.

The Revealing of the Antichrist (2:3)

The term "man of lawlessness" is a typical Hebraic construction where "man of..." refers to a close association.[270]

"Man of lawlessness" (NIV), "lawless one" (NRSV) describes the characteristic of the antichrist with the adjective *anomia*, "state or condition of being disposed to what is lawless, lawlessness," the opposite of *dikaisynē*, "righteous."[271]

In our verse, "the man doomed to destruction" (NIV), "one destined for destruction" (NRSV) is literally "the son of perdition" (KJV). The noun is *apōleia*, "loss," here, "the destruction that one experiences, both complete and in process, ruin."[272] Observe that in this case, *apōleia* does not mean complete annihilation, since their punishment lasts forever:

> "And the devil, who deceived them, was thrown into the lake of burning sulfur, where the beast and the false prophet had been thrown. They will be tormented day and night for ever and ever." (Revelation 20:10; cf. 19:20)

The Nature of the Antichrist (2:3-5)

Now Paul begins to describe the Antichrist and what he will do.

> "3 Don't let anyone deceive you in any way, for that day will not come until the rebellion occurs and the man of lawlessness is revealed, the man doomed to destruction. 4 He will oppose and will exalt himself over everything that is called God or is worshiped, so that he sets himself up in God's temple, proclaiming himself to be God." (2:3-4)

---

[270] *Anthrōpos*, with a qualifying genitive (BDAG 81, 4c). "Son of" refers to one whose identity is defined in terms of a relationship with a person or thing, denoting one who shares in it or who is worthy of it, or who stands in some other close relation to it. (*huios*, BDAG 1024, 2cβ).

[271] *Anomia*, BDAG 85, 1. This word is found in some of the best ancient Greek manuscripts, such as Aleph, B, 81, 88^mg 1739 cop^sa,bo arm, Marcion, Tertullian, etc. The KJV "man of sin" represents the Greek noun *hamartias*, "sin," which is supported by A, D, G it, vg, K, L, P and others. One of the ways scholars determine which is most likely the original text is what copyist scenario seems most likely. Here, Bruce Metzger concludes, "on the whole it appears that the early Alexandrian witnesses preserve the original reading *anomias*, a word rarely used by Paul, which was altered by copyists to the much more frequently used word, *hamartias*. Furthermore, "for the secret power of lawlessness" in verse 7 seems to presuppose *anomias* here." The Editorial Committee of the United Bible Societies' Greek New Testament give *anomias* a {C} rating, indicating some degree of uncertainty (Metzger, *Textual Commentary*, p. 635).

[272] The word is *apostasia* (from which we get our word "apostasy"). It means, "defiance of established system or authority, rebellion, abandonment, breach of faith," literally, "a falling away, defection, apostasy" (*apōleia*, BDAG 127, 2).

The Antichrist exhibits several characteristic actions to indicate that there will be no mistake about who he is. He is seeking to take God's rightful place.

1. **Lawless** (2:3). As we saw above, he rebels against God, becoming lawless – a law to himself.

2. **Rebels** (2:3b). He rebels against God – indeed he leads a worldwide rebellion or apostasy. So Christ won't return until *after* the Antichrist appears, and the "rebellion" (NIV, NRSV) or "falling away" occurs. [273] The Antichrist, the one opposed to God, leads a rebellion against God – the ultimate lawlessness!

3. **Opposes**[274] (2:4a). He will oppose any and every deity and religion, whether the true God or false gods.

4. **Exalts himself**[275] (2:4b). He will be characterized by pride, and will seek to exalt himself above all deities that are worshipped here on earth. He will allow no equals. In Paul's day, Roman emperors had declared themselves as gods, but this is something far greater.

5. **Takes his seat**[276] **in the temple of God** (2:4c), that is takes the place of God, whose presence in the temple was once indicated by the ark of the covenant.

6. **Proclaims**[277] **himself to be divine** (2:4d). He will not only take God's rightful place in the temple, he will announce to all that he is indeed God himself.

You'll find another description of the Antichrist in Revelation 13:1-10, where he is known as "the beast coming out of the sea." Here he is portrayed as a puppet of "the dragon," that is, Satan (Revelation 12:9), and will be promoted by the "false prophet," "the beast coming out of the earth," who carries out the Antichrist's orders. Revelation 13:3 tells us that the Antichrist had a "fatal wound" that had been healed, inspiring awe throughout the world, probably one of his counterfeit miracles.

> "The beast was given a mouth to utter proud words and blasphemies and to exercise his authority for forty-two months. He opened his mouth to blaspheme God, and to slander his name and his dwelling place and those who live in heaven. He was given power to

---

[273] *Apostasia*, Thayer 67, from *apo*, "from" + *stasis*, "standing, station, position, current state of affairs."

[274] "Oppose" (NIV) is *antikeimai*, "be opposed to someone, be in opposition to" (BDAG 89).

[275] "Exalts" is *hyperairō*, "to have an undue sense of one's self-importance, rise up, exalt oneself, be elated" (BDAG 1031). "Object of worship" (NRSV) is *sebasma*, "something that relates to devotional activity, devotional object." The word is used of Athenian idols (Acts 17:23).

[276] The verb is *kathizō*, "to take a seated position, sit down"(BDAG 492, 3).

[277] "Proclaims" is *apodeiknymi*, literally, "to 'point away' and 'direct attention' to a specific object. Here it means, "to show forth for public recognition as so and so, make, render, proclaim, appoint," especially as administrative term (BDAG 108, 1).

make war against the saints and to conquer them. And he was given authority over every tribe, people, language and nation. All inhabitants of the earth will worship the beast – all whose names have not been written in the book of life belonging to the Lamb that was slain from the creation of the world." (Revelation 13:5-8)

The Antichrist initiates a huge persecution against the church, since he is "allowed to make war on the saints and to conquer them" (Revelation 13:7). The Antichrist will try to force everyone to worship his image. They won't be allowed to buy and sell unless they are marked with the mark of the beast (Revelation 13:16-17). As Jesus told us:

> "If those days had not been cut short, no one would survive, but for the sake of the elect those days will be shortened." (Matthew 24:22)

According to Revelation 13:5-7, this period of the Antichrist is the second 3-1/2 year period of the seven years of tribulation. Whether this a literal or figurative period of time, I'll leave to those who love to speculate.

Q2. (2 Thessalonians 2:3-5; Revelation 13:5-8) What are the characteristics of the Antichrist that Paul gives in this passage? What does Revelation 13:5-8 add to our basic understanding?
http://www.joyfulheart.com/forums/index.php?showtopic=1245

The Restraint of the Antichrist (2:6-7)

Now Paul explains that something is restraining the Antichrist until he is finally revealed.

> "[6] And now you know what is holding him back, so that he may be revealed at the proper time. [7] For the secret power of lawlessness is already at work; but the one who now holds it back will continue to do so till he is taken out of the way." (2:6-7)

The word "holding back" (NIV), "restraining" (NRSV), "withholdeth" (KJV) is *katechō*, "to prevent the doing of something or cause to be ineffective, prevent, hinder, restrain," here, "to prevent someone from exercising power, restrain, check."[278] In verse

---

[278] *Katechō*, BDAG 533, 1c. Danker explains it as "what prevents God's adversary from coming out in open opposition to God, for the time being."

6 the Restrainer has a neuter gender, while in verse 7 the Restrainer seems to be a person (masculine gender). Paul had obviously explained all this to the Thessalonians when he was with them (verse 5). We can only wish that he had explained to *us* what the restraining force is. There are all sorts of speculations, which include:

1. The Roman Empire, or the principle of law and government, which characterized the Roman Empire (Romans 13:3-4). I think this is the most likely explanation.

2. Gospel preaching (Matthew 24:14),

3. The binding of Satan (Revelation 20:2),

4. The church,

5. The Holy Spirit,

6. An angel of God,

7. The Jewish state,

8. The providence of God, and

9. Michael the Archangel

I could present the arguments given for several of these positions, but, frankly, we just don't know who the Restrainer is. People's interpretations of this question depend a lot on their general interpretation of the end times. To speculate about it doesn't lead us to further truth. Like some other Bible questions to which we'd like an authoritative answer, this one will have to wait until we get to heaven.

The Overthrow of the Antichrist (2:8)

Now Paul explains that Christ's coming will precipitate the downfall of the Antichrist.

> "And then the lawless one will be revealed, whom the Lord Jesus will overthrow with the breath of his mouth and destroy by the splendor of his coming." (2:8)

Though the Antichrist will finally be revealed after the Restrainer is removed, he won't stay in power long. Soon after that, Christ will return and destroy him. Paul refers again to "the splendor of his coming" that he had described in 1:7-10. Christ will come with blazing fire, powerful angels, the majesty of his power, and his glory in his people.

According to the text, the Antichrist's downfall will come about by Christ's two-fold action:

1. **Overthrown by the breath of his mouth.**[279] Christ's power is so much greater, that when the time comes, Christ will literally "blow him away."

2. **Destroyed by the splendor of his coming.**[280] Christ will come with all the hosts of heaven and utterly destroy the Antichrist and his forces.

To get a full understanding of this mighty confrontation, you need to read out loud in Revelation of this awesome dramatic scene – heavy in symbolism – where Christ's forces are arrayed against those of the Antichrist ("the beast"). You can sense the drama and grandeur of Christ's victory and the Antichrist's downfall.

> "I saw heaven standing open and there before me was a **white horse**, whose rider is called **Faithful and True**. With justice he judges and makes war. His eyes are like blazing fire, and on his head are **many crowns**. He has a name written on him that no one knows but he himself. He is dressed in a **robe dipped in blood**, and his name is the **Word of God**. The **armies of heaven** were following him, riding on white horses and dressed in fine linen, white and clean. Out of his mouth comes a **sharp sword** with which to strike down the nations. 'He will rule them with an iron scepter.' He treads the winepress of the fury of the wrath of God Almighty. On his robe and on his thigh he has this name written: '**King of kings and Lord of lords.**'"

> "... Then I saw **the beast and the kings of the earth and their armies gathered together to make war** against the rider on the horse and his army. But the **beast was captured**, and with him the false prophet.... The two of them were **thrown alive into the fiery lake of burning sulfur.**" (Revelation 19:11-16, 19-20)

The Deceit of the Antichrist (2:9-10a)

However, while he is yet active, the Antichrist will perform all sorts of signs and wonders and succeed in deceiving the world. The Antichrist is a master of deception, learned from Satan himself.

---

[279] "Overthrow" (NIV), "destroy" (NRSV) is *anaireō/anelō*," to get rid of by execution, do away with, destroy someone," mostly of killing by violence, in battle, by execution, murder, or assassination" (BDAG 64, 2). The KJV translates a textual variant with "consume" (KJV), *analiskō*, "to do away with something completely by using up, destroy, consume" (BDAG 67). Metzger (*Textual Commentary*, p. 636) selects *anaireō/anelō* over *analiskō* chiefly on the quality of the external evidence (A B P 81 88 451).

[280] "Destroy" (NIV, KJV), "annihilating" (NRSV) is *katargeō*, "to cause something to come to an end or to be no longer in existence, abolish, wipe out, set aside" (BDAG 525, 3). "Splendor" (NIV), "manifestation" (NRSV), "brightness" (KJV) is *epiphaneia*. The basic meaning is "appearing, appearance," especially a "splendid appearance." As a technical term relating to transcendence it refers to a visible and frequently sudden manifestation of a hidden divinity, either in the form of a personal appearance, or by some deed of power or oracular communication by which its presence is made known (BDAG 386, 1b). The word "coming" is *parousia*, which we saw in 1 Thessalonians 2:19; 3:13; 4:15; and 2 Thessalonians 2:1 (BDAG 780, 2b).

"9 The coming[281] of the lawless one will be in accordance with the work[282] of Satan displayed in all kinds of counterfeit[283] miracles, signs and wonders, 10 and in every sort of evil that deceives[284] those who are perishing."[285] (2:9-10a)

Jesus himself had told his disciples to expect deceitful signs and wonders.

"For false Christs and false prophets will appear and perform great signs and miracles to deceive even the elect – if that were possible." (Matthew 24:24)

The Gullibility of the Deceived (2:10b-12)

How can people be so deceived? Paul explains the reason they are perishing.

"10b They perish because they refused[286] to love the truth and so be saved. 11 For this reason God sends them a powerful delusion[287] so that they will believe the lie 12 and so that all will be condemned[288] who have not believed the truth but have delighted in[289] wickedness." (2:10b-12)

It seems strange that the God of truth would encourage them to believe the lie. But this isn't the first time we see this. Twenty-five hundred years ago, Yahweh gave Isaiah this message – later quoted by Jesus as to why he spoke in parables:[290]

"'Be ever hearing, but never understanding;
be ever seeing, but never perceiving.'
Make the heart of this people calloused;

---

[281] "Coming" in 2:9 is *parousia*, the same word used to describe Jesus' coming.

[282] "Work/working" is *energeia*, "the state or quality of being active, working, operation, action, activity" (BDAG 335).

[283] "Counterfeit" (NIV), "lying" (NRSV, KJV) is *pseudos*, "a lie, falsehood" (BDAG 1097).

[284] "Evil that deceives" (NIV), "deceivableness of unrighteousness" (KJV) is better rendered "wicked deception" in the NRSV.

[285] "Perishing/perish" is *appollymi*, "perish, die," especially in the New Testament of eternal death (BDAG 116, 1bα). The present tense indicates that they are in the process of perishing right now.

[286] "Refused" (NIV, NRSV), "received not" (KJV) is two words, *ou*, "not" and *dechomai*, "receive," here it has the connotation, "to indicate approval or conviction by accepting, be receptive of, be open to, approve, accept" (BDAG 222, 5).

[287] "Delusion" is *planē* (from which we get our English word "planet," seen to be a "wandering" star) "wandering from the path of truth, error, delusion, deceit, deception" (BDAG 822). "Powerful" (NIV, NRSV), "strong" (KJV) is *energeia*, which we saw in verse 9. It is an active delusion, "a deluding influence" (BDAG 335).

[288] "Be condemned" (NIV, NRSV), "be damned" (KJV) is *krinō*, "select, judge," here with a negative connotation, "to engage in a judicial process, judge, decide, hale before a court, condemn, also hand over for judicial punishment," here with the emphasis on the verdict, "condemn, punish" (BDAG 568, 5bα).

[289] "Delighted" (NIV), "had/took pleasure" (NRSV, KJV) is *eudokeō*, "to take pleasure or find satisfaction in something, be well pleased, take delight," also, "delight in, like, approve" (BDAG 404, 2b).

[290] Matthew 13:13-15.

> make their ears dull and close their eyes.
> Otherwise they might see with their eyes,
> hear with their ears,
> understand with their hearts,
> and turn and be healed." (Isaiah 6:8-10)

The psalmist wrote:

> "But my people would not listen to me;
> Israel would not submit to me.
> So I gave them over to their stubborn hearts
> to follow their own devices." (Psalm 81:11-12)

Paul wrote something similar to the Roman church.

> "Since they did not think it worthwhile to retain the knowledge of God, he gave them over to a depraved mind, to do what ought not to be done." (Romans 1:28)

Though this is difficult for us to understand, it seems that people who reject the truth they are given, don't get an infinite number of chances. If we don't follow truth where it leads us, we will lose our ability to discern truth. This goes against our desire to never give up on people. Perhaps we take pride in being more tolerant than Jesus. But recall our Master's instructions to his disciples on their preaching mission:

> "If anyone will not welcome you or listen to your words, shake the dust off your feet when you leave that home or town. I tell you the truth, it will be more bearable for Sodom and Gomorrah on the day of judgment than for that town." (Matthew 10:14-15)

Jesus said:

> "This is the verdict: Light has come into the world, but men loved darkness instead of light because their deeds were evil. Everyone who does evil hates the light, and will not come into the light for fear that his deeds will be exposed. But whoever lives by the truth comes into the light, so that it may be seen plainly that what he has done has been done through God." (John 3:19-21)

When speaking about the heathen – and the Jew – Paul told the Roman church:

> "To those who by persistence in doing good seek glory, honor and immortality, he will give eternal life. But for **those who are self-seeking and who reject the truth and follow evil**, there will be wrath and anger." (Romans 2:7-8)

Pretty sobering words! Paul tells Timothy,

> "The Spirit clearly says that in later times some will abandon the faith and follow deceiving spirits and things taught by demons. Such teachings come through **hypocritical liars, whose consciences have been seared** as with a hot iron." (1 Timothy 4:1-2)

We make ourselves ripe for deception when we reject the truth and delight in wickedness, especially when we know in our heart of hearts that it is wrong. After a while, our grasp of the truth will have faded, our consciences will have been seared, and we are left believing our own lies. How sad! This is why we dare not put off responding to the call of God at the time he calls us.

> "Now is the acceptable time; see, now is the day of salvation!" (2 Corinthians 6:2, NRSV)

Q3. (2 Thessalonians 2:9-12) What makes people so gullible that they believe the Antichrist's deceptions? What is the reason that God gives them over to this deception? Why is a fearless seeking of God's truth so important to us? How can a preaching of the truth set people free?

http://www.joyfulheart.com/forums/index.php?showtopic=1246

Saved by God's Election, the Sanctifying Spirit, and Believing the Truth (2:13-14)

> "[13] But we ought always to thank God for you, brothers loved by the Lord, because from the beginning God chose you to be saved through the sanctifying work of the Spirit and through belief in the truth. [14] He called you to this through our gospel, that you might share in the glory of our Lord Jesus Christ." (2:13-14)

Both predestination and prevenient grace (God's grace that comes before man's decision) is seen here, especially if you accept the phrase "from the beginning" as being part of the earliest test.[291] Notice the three elements in our salvation. The first is the active cause, the second and third are the means:[292]

1. Active cause: God's choice or election "from the beginning" (*haireō*, "choose, prefer"). We weren't selected on the basis of our performance or action, but solely on the basis of his grace (1 Corinthians 2:7; Ephesians 2:8-9). As Paul wrote to Timothy:

---

[291] "From the beginning" (NIV, KJV, *ap' archēs*), "as the first fruits" (NRSV, *aparchēn*) indicate a textual variant in the early manuscripts. The difference in the Greek text is slight and Metzger, who prefers "from the beginning" over "as the first fruits," gives his preference only a {C} or "considerable degree of doubt" confidence level.

[292] These means are introduced by the preposition *en*, as a marker introducing means or instrument, "with" (BDAG 328, 5b).

"God ... has saved us and called us to a holy life – **not because of anything we have done** but because of **his own purpose and grace**. This grace was given us in Christ Jesus before the beginning of time...." (2 Timothy 1:9)

2. Means: the sanctifying work of the Spirit. The word is *hagiasmos* (which we've seen in 1 Thessalonians 2:13; 4:3-4, 7), "personal dedication to the interests of the deity, holiness, consecration, sanctification; the use in a moral sense for a process or, more often, its result (the state of being made holy)."[293]

"To God's elect ... who have been chosen according to the foreknowledge of God the Father, through **the sanctifying work** (*hagiasmos*) of the Spirit, for obedience to Jesus Christ and sprinkling by his blood." (1 Peter 1:1-2)

3. Means: belief in the truth. On God's side is election and the work of his Spirit. But on our side must be a belief in the truth. We must hold it tight and not let it go. God honors those who seek his truth.

"For God so loved the world that he gave his one and only Son, that **whoever believes in him** shall not perish but have eternal life." (John 3:16)

Hold Fast (2:15)

Paul has just finished talking about the deceptions of the Antichrist. The church has also been victim of some forged letter supposedly from Paul. So he winds down this section with an exhortation to hold fast the teachings he had given them.

"So then, brothers, stand firm and hold to the teachings we passed on to you, whether by word of mouth or by letter." (2:15)

Notice the powerful verbs that should encourage us also to hold fast to the Word of God that we have received.

- "**Stand firm**" (NIV, NRSV), "stand fast" (KJV) is *stēkō*, literally, "stand," figuratively, "to be firmly committed in conviction or belief, stand firm, be steadfast in something."[294]

- "**Hold fast**" (NRSV), "hold" (NIV, KJV), is *krateō*, "hold" with one's hands. Here it is used figuratively, "to adhere strongly to, hold, hold fast."[295]

As in Paul's day, so it is in ours. The teachings of Christ and the apostles have been watered down and distorted, corrupted by mixing them with various humanistic precepts and eastern religions. We must be determined to stand our ground and hold

---

[293] *Hagiasmos*, BDAG 10.
[294] *Stēkō*, BDAG 944, 2. Also in 1 Thessalonians 3:8.
[295] *Krateō*, BDAG 565, 6a.

the precious Word of God with steadfastness, boldness, and love. Especially love, so that we don't become defensive and withdrawn, but compassionate and outgoing, spreading the Word to all we know.

A Benediction of Hope, Strength, and Encouragement (2:16-17)

Now Paul prays for the church a beautiful benediction for encouragement, hope, and strength.

> "[16] May our Lord Jesus Christ himself and God our Father, who loved us and by his grace gave us eternal encouragement[296] and good hope, [17] encourage[297] your hearts and strengthen[298] you in every good deed and word." (2:16-17)

Protection from the Evil One (3:1-5)

Paul asks the church (*adelphoi*, "brothers" can also refer to "brothers and sisters") to pray for his ministry.

> "[1] Finally, brothers, pray for us that the message of the Lord may spread rapidly and be honored, just as it was with you. [2] And pray that we may be delivered from wicked[299] and evil[300] men, for not everyone has faith." (3:1-2)

He asks them to pray that the "message," literally, "the word,"[301] will "spread rapidly" (NIV, NRSV) or "have free course" (KJV). The verb is "run, rush, advance."[302] Paul is impatient. He wants to see the gospel surge past the obstacles that both the "evil one" and "wicked and evil men" put in the way to obstruct the furtherance of the gospel. We have those same enemies today. Paul asks prayer for deliverance[303] from these enemies

---

[296] "Encouragement" (NIV), "comfort" (NRSV), "consolation" (KJV) is *paraklēsis*, here, "lifting of another's spirits, comfort, consolation." In our verse "everlasting" = "inexhaustible" (BDAG 766, 3).

[297] "Encourage" (NIV), "comfort" (NRSV, KJV) is the corresponding verb, *parakaleō*, "to instill someone with courage or cheer, comfort, encourage, cheer up" (BDAG 765, 4).

[298] "Strengthen" (NIV, NRSV), "stablish" (KJV) is *stērizō*, literally, "set up, support," figuratively, "to cause to be inwardly firm or committed, confirm, establish, strengthen" (BDAG 945, 2). We see this word several times in 1 Thessalonians 3:2; 3:13 and 2 Thessalonians 3:3.

[299] "Wicked" (NIV, NRSV), "unreasonable" (KJV) is *atopos*, "out of place," here, "pertaining to being behaviorally out of place, evil, wrong, improper" (BDAG 149, 2).

[300] "Evil" (NIV, NRSV), "wicked" (KJV) is *ponēros*, "pertaining to being morally or socially worthless, wicked, evil, bad, base, worthless, vicious, degenerate" (BDAG 853, 1aα).

[301] "Message" (NIV), "word" (NRSV, KJV) is *logos*, "word." Here it refers to "the Christian message, the gospel" (BDAG 600, 1aβ).

[302] *Trechō*, BDAG 1015, 3. Here it has the figurative idea, "to proceed quickly and without restraint, progress."

[303] "Delivered" (NIV, KJV), "rescued" (NRSV) is *rhyomai*, "to rescue from danger, save, rescue, deliver, preserve someone" (BDAG 908).

of the gospel. And he asks prayer for receptivity,[304] the same kind of honor the Word had received in Thessalonica in the early days (1 Thessalonians 1:4-10). Notice the detailed way that he is teaching them to pray for the Christian mission.

Now he encourages their faith.

> "But the Lord is faithful, and he will strengthen[305] and protect[306] you from the evil one. " (3:3)

Jesus teaches his disciples to pray for this same protection and deliverance.

> "And lead us not into temptation,
> but deliver us from the evil one." (Matthew 6:13)

Finally, Paul expresses confidence in the Thessalonian believers that they will indeed obey what he has commanded and calls them to continued perseverance and love.

> "4 We have confidence[307] in the Lord that you are doing and will continue to do the things we command. 5 May the Lord direct[308] your hearts into God's love and Christ's perseverance." (3:4-5)

The ability to "hang in there" is essential. "Perseverance" (NIV), "steadfastness" (NRSV), "patient waiting" (KJV) is *hypomonē* (which we see in 1 Thessalonians 1:3 and 2 Thessalonians 1:4; 3:10), "the capacity to hold out or bear up in the face of difficulty, patience, endurance, fortitude, steadfastness, perseverance."[309]

If you've been around congregations very long, you know how important the quality of perseverance is. There are seasons of growth and joy and harvest. There are also seasons of difficulty and strife and decline. One important key to seeing Christ's church flourish is to persevere, to "hang in there," to stand in the face of difficulty. If your congregation is going through tough times right now, your perseverance is Christ's gift to move it towards health!

---

[304] "Be honored" (NIV), "be glorified" (NRSV, KJV) is *doxazō*, "praise, honor, extol" (BDAG 258, 2). Danker prefers a second definition for this verse: "to cause to have splendid greatness, clothe in splendor, glorify"), though I think the idea of "honor" is best here.

[305] "Strengthen" (NIV, NRSV), "stablish" (KJV) is *stērizō*, which we saw above in 2:17.

[306] "Protect" (NIV), "guard" (NRSV), "keep" (KJV) is *phylassō*, "to protect by taking careful measures, guard, protect" (BDAG 1068, 2b).

[307] "Confidence" is *peithō*, "convince," here, "to be so convinced that one puts confidence in something, depend on, trust in" (BDAG 792, 2a).

[308] "Direct" is *kateuthynō*, "'make/keep straight', lead, direct" (BDAG 532).

[309] *Hypomonē*, BDAG 1039, 1. Danker sees this as "Christ-like fortitude," that is, a fortitude that comes from association with Christ.

Q4. (2 Thessalonians 3:1-5) Why is perseverance so important as we see wickedness increasing? What happens if we stop believing and being patient? How can we help one another persevere? What part does faith and perseverance have in our salvation? What part does God's redemption and grace have in our salvation?
http://www.joyfulheart.com/forums/index.php?showtopic=1247

Lessons for Disciples

This lesson has been to teach disciples to patiently await Christ's return in spite of persecution and tribulation. Christ return will be preceded by the rise of the Antichrist, accompanied by a time of false signs and wonders and widespread persuasive deception. But, praise God, that evil man's reign will be gloriously interrupted by the coming of Christ, who will overthrow him, bring judgment, and set up the reign of the Son of Man and the Son of God that has been prophesied from of old:

> "He was given authority, glory and sovereign power;
> all peoples, nations and men of every language worshiped him.
> His dominion is an everlasting dominion that will not pass away,
> and his kingdom is one that will never be destroyed." (Daniel 7:14)

His kingdom is coming, even if all around you is the influence of antichrist spirits.

> "For the revelation awaits an appointed time;
> it speaks of the end and will not prove false.
> Though it linger, wait for it;
> it will certainly come and will not delay." (Habakkuk 2:3)

Until that time, dear friend, we follow the Apostle Paul's directive:

> "We have confidence in the Lord
> that you are doing
> and will continue to do the things we command.
> May the Lord direct your hearts into **God's love**
> and **Christ's perseverance**." (3:4-5)

Prayer

Father, thank you that the spirit of Antichrist that we see around us will not be the last word. We look forward to your coming, Lord Jesus! In the meantime, we ask for your grace that we might be faithful, obedient, and persevere – for your glory. In Christ's holy name, we pray. Amen.

Key Verses

"Don't let anyone deceive you in any way, for that day will not come until the rebellion occurs and the man of lawlessness is revealed, the man doomed to destruction. He will oppose and will exalt himself over everything that is called God or is worshiped, so that he sets himself up in God's temple, proclaiming himself to be God." (2 Thessalonians 2:3-4)

"And then the lawless one will be revealed, whom the Lord Jesus will overthrow with the breath of his mouth and destroy by the splendor of his coming." (2 Thessalonians 2:8)

"Finally, brothers, pray for us that the message of the Lord may spread rapidly and be honored, just as it was with you." (2 Thessalonians 3:1)

"But the Lord is faithful, and he will strengthen and protect you from the evil one." (2 Thessalonians 3:3)

9. Warning against Idleness (2 Thessalonians 3:6-18)

In 2 Thessalonians 3:1-5 it sounded like Paul was about to end his letter. But then it seems that he realizes that he must confront another issue that is disrupting the church – idleness.

The Thessalonian church has struggled with several problems, including persecution, a misunderstanding of Christ's coming, and lax sexual morals. But the problem of idleness didn't give way easily – overly dependent members who refused to work – in a word, "freeloaders."[310] They wanted a free ride without paying a fair share.

The problem was unsettling the church. These people had so much time on their hands that they were meddling in others' affairs (3:11) and causing problems, rather than living quiet lives providing for their families (3:12).

Congregations, particularly brand new ones, can become confused. We are told to love our neighbors as ourselves. We are told not to be judgmental. We are told to share all things in common. These are the principles. But where are the boundaries? What do we do when a believer takes advantage of the fellowship's generosity without contributing?

Commanded in the Name of the Lord Jesus Christ (3:6)

Paul had spoken to this situation twice in his first letter (1 Thessalonians 4:11-12 and 5:14), but the problem has persisted. In this second letter, Paul is no longer indirect, hoping that the loafers will get the point. Now he speaks with a clear command, speaking with the powerful authority of Jesus Christ himself!

> "In the name of the Lord Jesus Christ, we command you, brothers, to keep away from every brother who is idle and does not live according to the teaching you received from us." (3:6)

This phrase variously translated "idle" (NIV), "living in idleness" (NRSV), "walketh disorderly" (KJV) – both here and in verse 11 – is a combination of the verb *parapateō*, "walk, conduct oneself" and the adverb *ataktos*, which means, "not in the proper

---

[310] The English verb "freeload" is "to impose upon another's generosity or hospitality without sharing in the cost or responsibility involved" (*Merriam-Webster's 11th Collegiate Dictionary*).

order."[311] The related verb, *atakteō*, is found in verse 7. Originally, it referred to soldiers marching out of order or quitting the ranks, thus it has the idea of "to be neglectful of duty, to be lawless."[312]

Instead of doing their fair share to support themselves and help the poor in the Christian community, these idlers are lazy, hanging around other believers, and then expecting to be asked for dinner and given a place to sleep – night after night!

"Command" is a strong verb, *parangellō*, used here and in verses 10 and 12: "to make an announcement about something that must be done, give orders, command, instruct, direct." It is a word used by people in authority – worldly rulers, Jesus, the apostles, etc.[313]

Paul isn't talking about people who can't earn a living because of sickness, mental instability, age, or infirmity. He isn't talking about widows who have no support, or orphans whose parents have died. He's talking about people who could work, but don't.

Paul's command to the believers is to "keep away" from these lazy people. We'll consider this further when Paul expands on it in 3:14-15.

A Biblical Work Ethic

Paul isn't teaching a so-called "Protestant work ethic" here.[314] Rather he is teaching the concept of taking responsibility for oneself and one's family, a basic concept that is found throughout the Bible. Paul reiterates this concept to Timothy:

> "If anyone does not provide for his relatives, and especially for his immediate family, he
> has denied the faith and is worse than an unbeliever." (1 Timothy 5:8)

Paul ran across laziness elsewhere. In the church of Ephesus he gives instructions to former thieves: Get a job, do something productive, so that you may add to the community, not take away from it.

---

[311] *Ataktos* is sometimes used of soldiers who are out of the ranks. Here it is used in the sense of "being out of step and going one's own way, disorderly, insubordinate," or "idle, indolent" (BDAG 148, 1; Thayer 83.

[312] *Atakteō*, Thayer 812, b.

[313] *Parangellō*, BDAG 760.

[314] The concept of the "Protestant work ethic" was introduced by Max Weber, in his book *The Protestant Ethic and the Spirit of Capitalism* (1904). He argues that Protestants, beginning with Martin Luther, reconceptualized worldly work as a duty which benefits both the individual and society as a whole. According to Weber, the Catholic idea of good works in order to be saved, was transformed into an obligation to work diligently as a sign of grace, the consequence of an already-received salvation (Wikipedia).

"He who has been stealing must steal no longer, but must work, doing something useful with his own hands, that he may have something to share with those in need." (Ephesians 4:28)

Hard work is the norm laid out in Genesis:

"By the sweat of your brow you will eat your food...." (Genesis 3:19a)

The book of Proverbs especially is pretty hard on "sluggards." Here are some examples:

"Go to the ant, you sluggard;
consider its ways and be wise!" (Proverbs 6:6)

"Lazy hands make a man poor,
but diligent hands bring wealth.
He who gathers crops in summer is a wise son,
but he who sleeps during harvest is a disgraceful son." (Proverbs 10:4-5)

"The sluggard craves and gets nothing,
but the desires of the diligent are fully satisfied." (Proverbs 13:4)

"One who is slack in his work is brother to one who destroys." (Proverbs 18:9)

"The sluggard's craving will be the death of him,
because his hands refuse to work.
All day long he craves for more,
but the righteous give without sparing." (Proverbs 21:25-26)

"A sluggard does not plow in season;
so at harvest time he looks but finds nothing." (Proverbs 20:4)

"I went past the field of the sluggard,
past the vineyard of the man who lacks judgment;
thorns had come up everywhere,
the ground was covered with weeds,
and the stone wall was in ruins.
I applied my heart to what I observed
and learned a lesson from what I saw:
A little sleep, a little slumber, a little folding of the hands to rest –
and poverty will come on you like a bandit
and scarcity like an armed man." (Proverbs 24:30-34)

"The sluggard is wiser in his own eyes
than seven men who answer discreetly." (Proverbs 26:16)

"If a man is lazy, the rafters sag;
if his hands are idle, the house leaks." (Ecclesiastes 10:18)

Women, too, were responsible to do their share.

> "[The capable wife] watches over the affairs of her household
> and does not eat the bread of idleness." (Proverbs 31:27)

Paul advises Timothy not to put younger women on a list of widows who receive support from the church. Rather they should remarry. It's obvious by his comments that he's seen the result of idle women harming the church because they have too much time on their hands.

> "As for younger widows, do not put them on such a list.... They get into the habit of being idle[315] and going about from house to house. And not only do they become idlers, but also gossips and busybodies, saying things they ought not to." (1 Timothy 5:11, 13)

Paul teaches the same lessons to others. To the Ephesian elders, he said:

> "You yourselves know that these hands of mine have **supplied[316] my own needs and the needs of my companions**. In everything I did, I showed you that **by this kind of hard work we must help[317] the weak**, remembering the words the Lord Jesus himself said: 'It is more blessed to give than to receive.'" (Acts 20:34-35)

To the Corinthians he says,

> "We work hard with our own hands...." (1 Corinthians 4:12a)

For the believers in Crete, Paul instructed Titus:

> "Our people must learn to devote themselves to doing what is good, in order that they may **provide for daily necessities** and not live unproductive lives." (Titus 3:14)

The Bible is consistent here. We are to work so that we can care for our own needs, and for those who are weak and can't work. If we don't work, we can expect to pay the consequences, both naturally and socially.

Q1. (2 Thessalonians 3:6-15) What does the Bible teach about sloth and idleness among those who _can_ work but refuse to? Summarize it briefly. What is our Christian duty?
http://www.joyfulheart.com/forums/index.php?showtopic=1248

---

[315] "Idle" (which occurs twice in 1 Timothy 5:13) is _argos_, "pertaining to being without anything to do, unemployed, idle" (BDAG 128, 2).

[316] "Supplied" (NIV), "support" (NRSV), "ministered" (KJV) is _hypēreteō_, "to render service, serve, be helpful" (BDAG 1033).

[317] "Help" (NIV), "support" (NRSV, KJV), is _antilambanō_, "to take someone's part by assisting, take part, come to the aid of" (BDAG 89), from _anti-_, "requital " + _lambanō_, "receive," that is, "to take in turn or in return, to receive one thing for another given, to receive instead of" (Thayer 50). Or "to take hold yourselves (middle voice) at the other end (_anti_)" (Robertson, _Word Pictures_).

Paul's Example of Earning His Own Living (3:7-9)

Now in 2 Thessalonians (as he had in 1 Thessalonians 2:9), Paul teaches by his own example of working for his food, presumably as a tentmaker (Acts 18:3).

> "7 For you yourselves know how you ought to follow our example.[318] We were not idle when we were with you, 8 nor did we eat anyone's food without paying for it.[319] On the contrary, we worked night and day, laboring and toiling so that we would not be a burden to any of you. 9 We did this, not because we do not have the right to such help, but in order to make ourselves a model for you to follow." (2 Thessalonians 3:7-9)

One's own personal example is powerful. Paul's lifestyle was abundantly clear to the Thessalonian believers. Let's look at the elements of verse 8.

1. **"Toil"** (NIV), "labor" (NRSV, KJV), *kopos*, carries the idea "to engage in activity that is burdensome, work, labor, toil."[320]

2. **"Hardship"** (NIV), "toil" (NRSV), "travail" (KJV) is *mochthos*, "labor, exertion, hardship."[321] Robertson notes that it is an "old word for difficult labor, harder than *kopos* (toil)."[322]

3. **"Worked"** (NIV, NRSV), "laboring" (KJV) is *ergazomai*, "to engage in activity that involves effort, work."[323]

Hard work isn't to be avoided or to be ashamed of; it is part of the life of a disciple of Jesus!

Notice that in 3:9, Paul does not say that all apostles or Christian workers should support themselves! Let's not over interpret this.

> "We did this, not because we do not have the right[324] to such help, but in order to make ourselves a model for you to follow." (3:9)

His purpose is to give the believers an example or model[325] of hard work, not to set a precedent for all Christian workers. To the Corinthians he outlines the case for

---

[318] "Follow our example" (NIV), "imitate" (NRSV), "follow" (KJV) in verses 7 and 10 is *mimeomai*, "to use as a model, imitate, emulate, follow" (BDAG 652). From *mimos*, "imitator, mimic." (Our word "mimic" comes from this root.)

[319] "Without paying" (NIV, NRSV), "for nought" (KJV), is literally, "not as a gift."

[320] *Kopos*, BDAG 558, 2.

[321] *Mochthos*, BDAG 660.

[322] Robertson, *Word Pictures*.

[323] *Ergazomai*, BDAG 389, 1.

[324] "Right" (NIV, NRSV), "power" (KJV) is *exousia*, "authority, warrant." Here it has the nuance, "a state of control over something, freedom of choice, right" (BDAG 352, 1 and 3).

supporting Christian workers, and reserves his right to be supported for his work in the gospel, while choosing not to exercise it.

> "Don't we have the right to food and drink? Don't we have the right to take a believing wife along with us, as do the other apostles and the Lord's brothers and Cephas? ... If others have this right of support from you, shouldn't we have it all the more? But we did not use this right. On the contrary, we put up with anything rather than hinder the gospel of Christ." (1 Corinthians 9:4-5, 12)

Q2. (2 Thessalonians 3:7-9) What kind of example did Paul set with regard to work when he was in Thessalonica? As a Christian worker, did he have a right to support? Why didn't he exercise that right?

http://www.joyfulheart.com/forums/index.php?showtopic=1249

Paul's Rule: No Work, No Food (3:10)

Paul refers to his example while with them. Now he refers back to his teaching during his short time with the Thessalonians before being ejected from the city. Paul had taught the Bible doctrine of working hard to support one's family outlined above.

> "For even when we were with you, we gave you this rule: 'If a man will not work,[326] he shall not eat.'" (3:10)

Observe four things here.

1. **Persistent sin.** The problem of laziness had existed from the church's foundation – and Paul had taught about it then.

2. **Command.** Paul's instruction about work at the founding of the church wasn't just a suggestion, but a command.[327]

---

[325] "Model" (NIV), "example" (NRSV), "ensample" (KJV) is *typos*, which we saw in 1 Thessalonians 1:7, "an archetype serving as a model, type, pattern, model," in the moral life, "example, pattern" (BDAG 1019-1020, 6b).

[326] "Work" is *ergazomai*, in verse 10 and 11 which we saw above in 3:8b and 1 Thessalonians 2:9 – "to engage in activity that involves effort, work" (BDAG 389, 1).

[327] "Gave ... rule" (NIV), "gave ... command" (NRSV), "commanded" (KJV) is the verb *parangellō*, which we saw in verse 6 and appears again in verse 12.

3. **Willful sin.** The issue is obedience to the Biblical injunction. The lazy believers know what the Bible says, but resist it. The will[328] is at stake here. Paul isn't talking about those who can't find work, those who are homeless against their will, or who are physically or mentally unable to work, but those who have no intention of working to support themselves.

4. **Consequences of actions.** Paul commands the believers to step back from continually "bailing out" the lazy people, and let the consequences of their actions teach them what they won't learn otherwise. Don't feed them – and don't feel guilt about it yourself!

Q3. (2 Thessalonians 3:10) If we were to follow Paul's rule, "If a man will not work, he shall not eat," wouldn't that allow people to starve? It sounds harsh. What are the positive results of this rule? To whom in a Christian community would this rule apply. To whom would it *not* apply?
http://www.joyfulheart.com/forums/index.php?showtopic=1250

Don't Be Busybodies, but Work Quietly (3:11)

Now Paul makes it clear that to allow this lazy dependency to continue hurts the church:

> "[11] We hear that some among you are idle. They are not busy; they are busybodies. [12] Such people we command and urge in the Lord Jesus Christ to settle down and earn the bread they eat. [13] And as for you, brothers, never tire of doing what is right." (3:11-13)

The laziness is causing two problems in the body.

1. Lazy people become busybodies and meddlers who hurt relationships in the body. Verse 11b includes a play on words that the NIV captures to some extent:

> "They are not busy (*ergazomai*); they are busybodies (*periergazomai*)."

---

[328] "Will not" (NIV), "unwilling" (NRSV), "would not" (KJV) is two words: *ou*, "not" and the verb *thelō*, "desire," here, "to have something in mind for oneself," of purpose, resolve, "will, wish, want, be ready" to do something (BDAG 448, 2).

"Busybodies" is *periergazomai*, "to be intrusively busy, be a busybody, meddler."[329] Thayer defines it, "to bustle about uselessly, to busy oneself about trifling, needless, useless matters."[330]

Later in his ministry, Paul sees the same problem of busybodies in Ephesus among young widows with time on their hands.[331]

The situation at Thessalonica is serious and must be fixed. That's why Paul can't just hint at a solution. So in verse 12, Paul both uses two strong verbs, "we command (*parangellō*) and urge ("exhort," KJV, NRSV, *parakaleō*) in the Lord Jesus Christ" (cf. 3:1, 10). The command is:

"To settle down and earn the bread they eat." (3:12b)

The phrases "settle down and earn" (NIV), "work quietly" (NRSV), "with quietness work" (KJV) translate three words: the verb *ergazomai*, "work" (which we've seen several times in this passage), the preposition *meta*, "with," and the noun *hēsychia*, "state of quietness without disturbance, quietness, rest," that is, living in a way that does not cause disturbance.[332] I think that the NIV's "settle down and earn" catches the idea well. These lazy people are stirring up others with their gossipy, busybody behavior. People resent them. The church is disturbed about it. So the lazy people are commanded to begin to work and stop stirring things up. As they begin to work, the dissension in the body will quiet down.

2. Lazy people can "burn out" or discourage church members from being generous and outgoing to the truly needy. The great majority of the believers at Thessalonica, no doubt, earn their own living, but have been putting up with the Christian freeloaders for far too long. They're tired of it. They've worn themselves out trying to do the "loving" thing. Paul wants to encourage them keep on doing good works – just not to enable the lazy believers among them.

"And as for you, brothers, never tire of doing what is right." (3:13)

---

[329] *Periergazomai*, BDAG 800.

[330] *Periergazomai*, Thayer 502. The preposition *peri-* that makes the compound verb carries the idea, "'beyond,' because that which surrounds a thing does not belong to the thing itself but is beyond it" (Thayer 502, III, 2). Liddell-Scott sees the basic sense as "take more pains than enough about a thing, waste one's labor on it," with our sense following, "meddle with, be a busybody."

[331] "They get into the habit of being idle and going about from house to house. And not only do they become idlers, but also gossips and busybodies, saying things they ought not to" (1 Timothy 5:13). "Idle" is *argos* "pertaining to being without anything to do, unemployed, idle" (BDAG 128, 1). "Gossips" (NIV, NRSV), "tattlers" (KJV) is *phlyaros*, "gossipy," from *phlyō*, "to babble" (BDAG 1060).

[332] *Hēsychia*, BDAG 446, 1.

"Never tire" (NIV), "do not be weary" (NRSV, cf. KJV) is *ekkakeō*, "lose heart,"[333] literally, "to be utterly spiritless, to be wearied out, exhausted."[334] Elsewhere, the New Testament exhorts people not to let discouragement immobilize them:

> "Therefore, since through God's mercy we have this ministry, we **do not lose heart**." (2 Corinthians 4:1)

> "I ask you, therefore, **not to be discouraged** because of my sufferings for you, which are your glory." (Ephesians 3:13)

> "Therefore **we do not lose heart**. Though outwardly we are wasting away, yet inwardly we are being renewed day by day." (2 Corinthians 4:16)

> "Consider him who endured such opposition from sinful men, so that you will **not grow weary and lose heart**." (Hebrews 12:3)

"Doing what is right" (NIV, NRSV), "well doing" (KJV)[335] in 3:13 has two aspects in Paul's writings:

(a) Charitable acts to help the needy, following the example of Christ and Paul himself. Jesus taught in the Parable of the Sheep and the Goats:

> "I was hungry and you gave me something to eat, I was thirsty and you gave me something to drink, I was a stranger and you invited me in, I needed clothes and you clothed me, I was sick and you looked after me, I was in prison and you came to visit me.... I tell you the truth, whatever you did for one of the least of these brothers of mine, you did for me." (Matthew 25:35-36, 40)

Paul told the Ephesian elders,

> "In everything I did, I showed you that by this kind of hard work we must help the weak, remembering the words the Lord Jesus himself said: 'It is more blessed to give than to receive.'" (Acts 20:35)

Paul tells the Galatian church,

> "Let us not become weary (*ekkakeō*) in doing good, for at the proper time we will reap a harvest if we do not give up."[336] (Galatians 6:9)

---

[333] *Ekkakeō*, BDAG 303.

[334] *Ekkakeō*, Thayer 195. This is a compound verb from *ek-*, here with the idea of "utterly, entirely" (*ek*, Thayer, 192, VI, 6) + *kakos*, "to be bad or weak," by implication, to fail in heart, faint, be weary (Strong).

[335] "Doing what is right" (NIV, NRSV), "well doing" (KJV) is the verb *kalopoieō*, "do what is right, good" (BDAG 504). It is a compound verb from "do" + "good." More often, the thought is expressed by Paul with the verb *poieō* and the neuter of the adjective or pronoun *agathos*, "good" (high worth, value)" or *kalos*, "good" (high level of usefulness) (*poieō*, BDAG 840, 2e).

[336] "Do not give up" (NIV, NRSV), "faint not" (KJV) in Galatians 6:9 is *eklyō*, "be exhausted in strength, become weary, give out" (BDAG 306).

(b) Earning a living *so* you can support your families. Observe how Paul uses the idea in his letter to Titus:

> "Our people must learn to devote themselves to doing what is good, *in order that* they may provide for daily necessities and not live unproductive lives." (Titus 3:14)

Do Not Associate with Lazy Believers (3:14-15)

When Paul began this section of the letter, he commanded in no uncertain terms:

> "In the name of the Lord Jesus Christ, we command you, brothers, to keep away from every brother who is idle and does not live according to the teaching you received from us." (3:6)

Paul commands a sort of shunning of the lazy believers who disobey Paul's directive. In verse 6, "keep away" (NIV, NRSV), "withdraw yourselves" (KJV) is *stellō*, "to keep one's distance, keep away, stand aloof."[337] In verses 14-15 he explains what this partial shunning should consist of.

> "¹⁴ If anyone does not obey our instruction in this letter, take special note of him. Do not associate with him, in order that he may feel ashamed. ¹⁵ Yet do not regard him as an enemy, but warn him as a brother." (3:14-15)

Paul's instruction, his command, has three elements:

1. **Identify the lazy believers.** The first step to solving a problem is to define it – in this case, note who exactly fits in this category. Perhaps this "marking"[338] was done in a public meeting of the congregation, or maybe by the leaders who passed the word. There are "givers" and there are "takers." The Christian community is a giving fellowship. Perpetual takers don't fit very well.

2. **Don't associate with these lazy believers.** The verb means, "mingle, associate with."[339] This is similar to the command to "keep one's distance" in verse 6. The purpose here is not punitive, but to make the lazy person be ashamed of what he is doing. We are not to treat lazy believers as enemies – they are family, they are

---

[337] *Stellō*, BDAG 942, 1. In Homer and other ancient Greek literature it is used in the active sense, "make ready, send" (as in the root of *apostellō*, "to send"). But in the New Testament and the Septuagint *stellō* is only in the middle voice. In ancient Greek you see the sense, "gather up, make compact," especially as a nautical term, "furl, take in." In a medical sense it can mean "restrict one's diet," also, "avoid," which is the idea in our verse and 2 Corinthians 8:20 (Liddell-Scott, IV, 4).

[338] "Take note" (NIV, NRSV), "note" (KJV) is *sēmeioō*, "note down, write." Here it is used figuratively, "to take special notice of, mark" (BDAG 923, 2).

[339] *Synanamignymi*, BDAG 965. Literally, the compound verb means "to mix up together." From *syn-*, "with" + *ana-*, "over again" + *mignumi*, "mix, mingle."

brothers. Paul says, "Yet do not regard him as an enemy, but warn him as a brother" (3:15). This isn't as severe a shunning as Paul calls for in Corinth, where a brother was openly and flagrantly sleeping with his step-mother (1 Corinthians 5:9, 11).[340] The Amish shunning that we sometimes hear about goes to the extent of not even talking to or doing business with a person who is shunned by the community. Paul doesn't intend that extent of shunning here.

3. **Warn these lazy believers**. The verb means, "to counsel about avoidance or cessation of an improper course of conduct, admonish, warn, instruct."[341] The elders, who are charged with admonishing and correcting (1 Thessalonians 5:12) are probably the ones to do the warning and provide instruction to the lazy believers about how they can regain their status in the community.

I would guess that the shunning in Thessalonica was designed to be mild but clear. You can't come to our fellowship meals. We won't "hang out" with you. When you come by the house to gab, you're turned away politely with, "We're busy working. We don't have time to talk right now." When a lazy believer shows up at dinner time, he is politely but firmly told, "We can't have you for dinner. You know what the leaders of church have said about this...."

Church disciple is difficult to exercise in what is designed to be a community of love. But when exercised lovingly, firmly, and consistently, it can have the effect of removing problems that otherwise stir up and discourage the fellowship. Paul commands the community to do this – and if they will, they'll be healed. I've observed churches that have no discipline or which are afraid to exercise discipline. Believe me, the lack of disciple is *not* better! The failure to exercise appropriate and timely discipline is one of the reasons that some of our Christian communities are unhealthy and have stopped growing.

Q4. (2 Thessalonians 3:9-16) Why do so many churches avoid exercising any church discipline? What is the result of a thoughtful and appropriate application of church discipline? What is the result of neglect of church discipline?
http://www.joyfulheart.com/forums/index.php?showtopic=1251

---

[340] Karl H. Rengstorf (*sēmeion, ktl.*, TDNT, 200-269) comments, "The shunning probably applies to spiritual fellowship or common meals, not to everyday matters."
[341] *Noutheteō*, BDAG 679.

Lessons for Disciples

What are we disciples supposed to learn from this? Paul is encouraging the church to get back on track and not let these lazy people disrupt, discourage, or embitter the group. He exhorts them not to grow weary in doing good – only to grow wiser.

A congregation, particularly a smaller congregation, can be like an extended family. Healthy families have a way of exercising a degree of discipline. "Uncle Ernie is always dropping in just at dinner time. Next time, don't invite him in." Erring family members aren't invited to family gatherings or parties. Eventually, they get the idea. Either I conform to the standards of this family, or I won't be able to enjoy being part of it. Uncle Ernie isn't treated as a enemy, only he is no longer welcome at meals and to stay the night.

Here are the guidelines given us in the New Testament:

1. Care for your family members so they don't become dependent upon the church. If you have aged, infirm, or mentally-challenged family members, you take care of them. That's only right.

2. Everybody who can is expected to do their share to make the family work. Each has different jobs and responsibilities, but each is important to the welfare of the whole.

3. If a widow or orphan has no family who can take care of them, the congregation can take on that responsibility, but only for those who clearly are unable to take care of themselves. Otherwise, they're expected to remarry or get some kind of job to earn their keep.

4. If members of the Christian community push these boundaries consistently and become dependent on others, they are to be identified, warned, and kept at a distance until they change their ways.

Of course, Paul's letters are designed to guide Christian communities, not cities, states, or nations. But, if you think about it, most provisions for a "social safety net" follow these guidelines. To the degree that our laws encourage dependency by those who can work and contribute to society, they are either bad laws or administered poorly.

Concluding Words (3:16-18)

Paul concludes the body of the letter with a brief benediction or prayer of blessing for his readers:

> "Now may the Lord of peace himself give you peace at all times and in every way. The
> Lord be with all of you." (3:16)

For a church that is under persecution from without and dissention about caring for freeloaders from within, Paul prays that Christ will give them peace.

As you may recall, someone trying to "deceive" (2:3a) the church may have sent a "prophecy, report or letter supposed to have been from us saying that the day of the Lord has already come" (2:2). So in this letter, Paul says:

> "I, Paul, write this greeting in my own hand, which is the distinguishing mark in all my
> letters. This is how I write." (3:17)

An amanuensis or secretary probably penned the letter as Paul dictated, but the apostle adds a sentence at the very end in his own handwriting to give the Thessalonians assurance that the letter is authentic.

Paul concludes this letter, as he did in 1 Thessalonians and most epistles, with a benediction of grace:

> "The grace of our Lord Jesus Christ be with you all." (3:18)

Paul began the letter wishing them grace and peace (1:2). And so he concludes, with a prayer for grace, the unmerited favor of God released through Jesus Christ's death for our sins, our steadfast and sure hope for our futures – grace.

Prayer

Father, give us wisdom in our churches how to help people in tangible ways without making them dependent. We ask for your grace for people who have been laid off or can't find work. Help your people get good jobs so that they may be a blessing to those less fortunate. Lord, we are utterly dependent upon you. Help us. In Jesus' name, we pray. Amen.

Key Verses

> "For even when we were with you, we gave you this rule: 'If a man will not work, he
> shall not eat.'" (2 Thessalonians 3:10)

> "Now may the Lord of peace himself give you peace at all times and in every way. The
> Lord be with all of you." (2 Thessalonians 3:16)

Appendix 1. Can Heathen Who Have Never Heard the Gospel Be Saved?

The question of whether heathen who haven't heard of Jesus will be saved isn't really treated in 2 Thessalonians 1:8-9. But since Paul talks about terrible judgment upon unbelievers, the question is present in the minds of many modern-day readers nevertheless. If God condemns people to hell, is it fair to send people to hell who have never had a chance of being saved?

An Outline of How the Heathen Might Be Saved

I encourage you to purchase a book on Christian apologetics to study a more thorough discussion of the question. But let me outline the elements of what I believe is a Biblical but tentative answer. What happens to the heathen isn't fully clear in Scripture. But we know that:

1. Justice. God is just, which means that he will judge all people fairly (Genesis 18:25; Psalm 145:17).

2. Love. God loves the world (John 3:16) and desires all people to be saved (2 Peter 3:9; 1 Timothy 2:4; Ezekiel 33:11).

3. General Revelation. God has revealed some basic truths about himself to all mankind (known as "general revelation").

> "What may be known about God is plain to them, because God has made it plain to them. For since the creation of the world God's invisible qualities – his eternal power and divine nature – have been clearly seen, being understood from what has been made, so that **men are without excuse.**" (Romans 1:19-20)

> "The heavens declare the glory of God;
> the skies proclaim the work of his hands.
> Day after day they pour forth speech;
> night after night they display knowledge.
> There is no speech or language
> where their voice is not heard.
> Their voice goes out into all the earth,
> their words to the ends of the world." (Psalms 19:1-4a)

In a sense, those who acknowledge and believe this general revelation can be said to "know God" (as it says in Romans 1:21, 28; and Acts 14:17). People can either accept and act on these basic truths, or reject them, distort them, and suppress them.

It is vital to understand that, while general revelation is only bare-bones information, nevertheless it is enough information on which people can act – and God holds them responsible for this revelation. People are without excuse!

4. Natural Law. God has also given mankind a conscience, a sense of justice, a general guide to right and wrong, a natural law. Many sins are obvious to everyone (Galatians 5:19-21). Paul wrote:

> "When Gentiles, who do not have the law, do by nature things required by the law, they are a law for themselves, even though they do not have the law, since they show that the requirements of the law are **written on their hearts**, their **consciences** also bearing witness, and their thoughts now accusing, now even defending them." (Romans 2:14-15)

The problem, of course, is man's bent to sinning – and the existence of a tempter who hates God and the knowledge of God. Unfortunately, we are not consistently rational beings. We tend to deceive ourselves and others (1 Corinthians 3:18; 6:9; Job 15:31; Obadiah 3). Too often, we suppress the truth we know when we don't want to act on it (Romans 1:18-19[342]). For many, becoming a Christian is not so much an intellectual challenge, as a moral challenge. Many so-called "seekers" don't want to repent and do what they know they should; thus can't be saved.

5. Sin. All have sinned (Romans 3:23), and though all sin is serious (James 2:10), there seem to be degrees of sins – some greater, some less (Matthew 23:23; John 19:11; Luke 12:47-48; Matthew 12:31-32; Romans 3:25).

6. Light. We are judged on the basis of the light we are given. Those who don't know much are responsible to do only for what they know to do. Those who know much have a greater responsibility (1 Timothy 1:13; Romans 2:13-15; 5:15; Acts 17:30-31). "From everyone who has been given much, much will be demanded" (Luke 12:48b).

7. Jesus' Redemption. Christ's salvation through his death on the cross provides the basis for redemption of any person – past, present, and future – though we know that not all will be saved. Jesus is mankind's only hope. As he said,

> "I am the way and the truth and the life.
> No one comes to the Father except through me." (John 14:6)

---

[342] "Suppress" (NIV, NRSV), "hold" (KJV) in Romans 1:18 is *katechō*, "to hold back, detain, retain," here, "to restrain, hinder." (Thayer, 1a).

"The Son of Man did not come to be served, but to serve,
and to give his life as a ransom for many." (Mark 10:45)

"This is a trustworthy saying that deserves full acceptance ... that we have put our hope in the living God, who is the Savior of all men, and especially of those who believe." (1 Timothy 4:9-10)

8. Salvation. Thus, Abraham and other Old Testament saints were saved by means of Christ's atonement, even though Abraham had not received a revelation of Jesus Christ. Christ's redemption is effective for Abraham's salvation, and perhaps others who believed in and followed the light they had.

"To those who by persistence in doing good seek glory, honor and immortality, he will give eternal life." (Romans 2:7)

The Bible isn't clear about all this. We are given hints, but not the full story about how the heathen might be saved, so I'm not trying to be dogmatic. Notice that I do *not* support universalism, that all humans will ultimately be saved. That is clearly false.

However, there are enough hints to suggest that it is *possible* for the heathen to be saved, so we can't accuse God of being unfair to people who have never heard. They have been given general revelation and are responsible. They have no excuse.[343]

So Why Preach the Gospel at All?

But if it *might* be possible for people to be saved without hearing about Christ, why should we preach the gospel to them? Doesn't preaching them the gospel give them a chance to reject Christ, which would result in them *not* being saved?

General revelation is only a general pointer to God. It reveals the existence of God and a basic sense of right and wrong, but doesn't provide a clear path to salvation. In fact, usually with only general revelation, people tend to reject God and instead worship the creation and creatures instead of the Creator himself (Romans 1:21-25). As Jesus said,

"Wide is the gate and broad is the road that leads to destruction,
and many enter through it.
But small is the gate and narrow the road that leads to life,
and only a few find it." (Matthew 7:13b-14)

So many are left in their sins, lost and confused.

"Jesus ... had compassion on them, because they were like sheep without a shepherd. So he began teaching them many things." (Mark 6:34)

---

[343] This argument follows the general approach of Dan Story, *Defending Your Faith: How to Answer the Tough Questions* (Nelson, 1992), pp. 121-129.

For this reason, we're commanded to evangelize (Matthew 28:18-20; Mark 16:15-16; Luke 24:47-48; Acts 1:8), to tell the story of Jesus our Savior, who loved us so much that he was willing to die for us. As Paul explains:

> "How, then, can they call on the one they have not believed in? And how can they believe in the one of whom they have not heard? And how can they hear without someone preaching to them? And how can they preach unless they are sent? As it is written, 'How beautiful are the feet of those who bring good news!'" (Romans 10:14-15, quoting Isaiah 52:7)

Over the centuries, as men and women have faithfully preached the compelling story of God's love and the God-man Jesus Christ, millions have put their faith in him and found abundant life – and eternal life!

God has given a witness of himself in creation and in the human conscience so that people may know him – repent of their sins, and seek him. We are all without excuse before a just God.

But man in his lostness and brokenness needs a Savior, a Physician who will come to him, heal his sin-sick soul, and give him eternal life. That Savior is Jesus, whom we proclaim with joy and love.

Appendix 2. How Can There Be a Hell Like the Bible Describes?

Second Thessalonians 1:9 talks about terrible judgment for those who reject Christ. In response to Biblical teaching about judgment, people often ask a difficult question: "How can there be a hell like the Bible describes?" While we can't cover the entire subject here, let me sketch the outlines of a response to this question.

Christian apologists Peter Kreeft and Ronald K. Tacelli note that, "Of all the doctrines in Christianity, hell is probably the most difficult to defend, the most burdensome to believe, and the first to be abandoned."[344] That doesn't mean, however, that it isn't true. They observe that if there were no hell:

1. Both Scripture and the church lie, for both clearly teach the reality of hell.

2. Jesus himself must be a liar, for he was more explicit than anyone else in the Bible.

3. We can change whatever doctrines we find unbearable or unacceptable.[345]

If hell is true, then many other belief systems must be false. These include:

1. Universalism or universal salvation.

2. Hell is only in this life.

3. Souls aren't eternal; they can be annihilated.

4. Reincarnation.

5. Hell is temporary.

6. Hell is empty.[346]

These beliefs must be false, but we must assert that:

1. God is *not* primarily a God of wrath, vengeance, and hate.

2. Hell is *not* forced on the damned. Rather, God respects our freedom of choice.

---

[344] Peter Kreeft and Ronald K. Tacelli, *Handbook of Christian Apologetics* (InterVarsity Press, 1994), p. 282.
[345] Kreeft and Tacelli, *Handbook*, p. 283.
[346] Kreeft and Tacelli, *Handbook*, pp. 285-289.

3. God's creation does *not* require a hell. Rather it was caused by rebellion and disobedience of angels and humans, not by God. God doesn't will damnation on anyone (Matthew 18:14).[347]

4. Some say that we can't have eternal joy in heaven if we know that friends we had on earth are in hell. But that presupposes a lot of things about hell that the Bible doesn't teach.

Kreeft and Tacelli argue that:

1. The punishment of hell is inevitable by natural law. If you reject the true God, the Source of all life, and his Savior Jesus Christ, then you naturally find death and misery as your inevitable punishment.

2. If God is the source of love and joy in reality, then our rejection of him should result in pain and joylessness.

3. Hell is privation, or deprivation of God.[348] It is "outer darkness where there is weeping and gnashing of teeth." It is being "shut out from the presence of the Lord and from the majesty of his power." (2 Thessalonians 1:9)

In the short scope of this lesson we can't develop all these arguments – but they are powerful. To learn more, consult a book on Christian apologetics.

---

[347] Kreeft and Tacelli, *Handbook*, pp. 289-292.
[348] Kreeft and Tacelli, *Handbook*, pp. 292-295.

Appendix 3. Participant Handout Guides

If you are working with a class or small group, feel free to duplicate the following handouts at no additional charge. If you'd like to print 8-1/2" x 11" or A4 size pages, you can download the free Participant Guide handout sheets at:

www.jesuswalk.com/thessalonians/thessalonians-lesson-handouts.pdf

Discussion Questions

You'll typically find 4 to 5 questions for each lesson, depending on the topics in each lesson. Each question may include several sub-questions. These are designed to get group members engaged in discussion of the key points of the passage. If you're running short of time, feel free to skip questions or portions of questions.

1. The Secret of Bountiful Believers (1 Thessalonians 1:1-10)
2. The Character of a Disciple-Maker (1 Thessalonians 2:1-16)
3. The Warm Heart of a Disciple-Maker (1 Thessalonians 2:17-3:13)
4. The Command and Blessing of Holy Sex (1 Thessalonians 4:1-12)
5. The Wonder and Warning of Christ's Return (1 Thessalonians 4:13-5:11)
6. Keys to a Healthy Christian Community (1 Thessalonians 5:12-28)
7. Awesome Judgment at Christ's Coming (2 Thessalonians 1:1-12)
8. The Coming Antichrist (2 Thessalonians 2:1-3:5)
9. Warning against Idleness (2 Thessalonians 3:6-18)

Because of the length of the these handouts – and to keep down the page count so we can keep the book price lower – they are being made available at no cost online. www.jesuswalk.com/thessalonians/thessalonians-lesson-handouts.pdf

CPSIA information can be obtained at www.ICGtesting.com
Printed in the USA
LVOW110135150113

315736LV00005B/141/P